T0150646

Editorial Director	Douglas Amrine
Editors	Grissarin Chungsiriwat and Nicholas Grossman
Contributors	Parisa Pichitmarn, Nick Koleszar, Lindsay Davis, Naomi Jane Goh and William Bredesen
Illustrator	Kathy MacLeod
Designer	Lisa Damayanti
Production Manager	Sin Kam Cheong

Editions Didier Millet Pte Ltd
Suite 707, 7th Floor, Panawongs Building
104 Surawong Road
Bangkok 10500, Thailand
Tel: +66(0)2 238 1570
E-mail: edm@edmbooks.com.sg

Website: www.edmbooks.com

First published in 2012

Printed by Tien Wah Press, Singapore

ISBN 978-981-4385-26-8

THAILAND
at RANDOM

THAILAND *at* RANDOM

edm EDITIONS DIDIER MILLET

In front of the house on Sukhumvit …
Cars rush by, causing headache.
The cars all move at a very high speed.
Flying cars in the sky also whizz past the house …
And then everybody sees a big train on Sukhumvit Road.
It looks like two trams attached, on rails, 10 metres above the road.
Its speed can't be less than 60 kilometres per hour …
Bangkok has more than 200 universities
And more than 5,000 primary and secondary schools.
No one needs to pay tuition.
Schools cover the costs of stationery, textbooks and even uniforms …
Every Bangkokian has an English name
Like Udom Robinson or Chatchawal Crawford.
We simply adapted ourselves and our culture
To be the same as our amicable American friends …
The current government has a civilian prime minister
Named Mr Issara Stewart.
Our Cabinet members are all civilians,
Even the minister of defence …

−translated excerpt from a chapter in P. Intrapalit's *Sam Kluea*
series in which the protagonists journey by time machine
to Bangkok in 2007. It was written in 1967.

RIDING THROUGH HISTORY
· · · · · · ·

Type of vehicle	First appearance	Key development
rot lak or *rot jek* (rickshaw)	Presented to King Chulalongkorn in 1871 by a Chinese merchant.	It was primarily a mode of public transportation operated by Chinese immigrants. In 1901, regulations were introduced to limit their number.
samlor (three-wheeled pedicab)	Invented in 1933 by Luean Pongsophon as a combination of the rickshaw and bicycle.	Due to a surge in the number of cars and motorcycles, the *samlor* was decommissioned in Bangkok and neighbouring Thonburi in 1968.
tuk-tuk (motorised three-wheeled pedicab)	Imported from Japan in 1959 to replace the *samlor*.	In Bangkok, they can no longer be registered. An estimated 7,405 remain in operation in the capital and 30,000 across the country.
taxi	Introduced briefly in 1925 but withdrawn as the fares were too expensive for most commuters.	Reintroduced to Bangkok in 1947. In 1958, an unsuccessful attempt was made to introduce meters. Without meters, taxi drivers charged flat rates, which were inconsistent and meant that passengers needed to bargain, often resulting in traffic jams. Meters were finally introduced in 1992.

ANATOMY OF FOOT REFLEXOLOGY
• • • • • • •

Chinese foot reflexology involves applying pressure to the patient's feet using the thumb, finger and hand as well as various tools and instruments. The underlying belief is that the body is reflected on the feet, which can be divided into different zones corresponding to various parts of the human anatomy. By applying pressure to these areas, the reflexologist can assess and improve the patient's health.

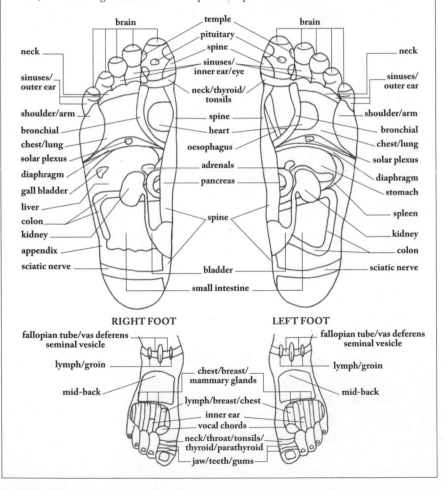

SIAM VERSUS THAILAND
· · · · · · ·

Since the reign of King Mongkut (r. 1851–1868), the country had been officially known as Siam. ("Siam" is believed to derive from the Portuguese translation of the Chinese word for the famous kingdom of Ayudhya, "Hsien".) In 1939, during the premiership of Field Marshal Pibul Songgram, however, the official name was changed to the Kingdom of Thailand before reverting to Siam after World War II during the term of Prime Minister Seni Pramoj. The three prime ministers who followed Seni all retained the name Siam. However, in 1949, after much contentious debate, and with Pibul again prime minister, the name Thailand, which means "Land of the Free", once again won the day. Those in favour of it argued the name encouraged patriotism. To this day, some academics and elder public figures wistfully wish for a return to the name Siam.

TALLEST BUILDINGS OVER TIME
· · · · · · ·

Building	Year of completion	Height
Ched Chan Building (in Chinatown)	1920	7 storeys
Kao Chan Building (in Chinatown)	1946	9 storeys
Chokchai Tower (in Sukhumvit)	1965	26 storeys
Bangkok Bank Building (in Silom)	1982	32 storeys (126 metres)
Jewelry Trade Center (in Silom)	1996	59 storeys (220.7 metres)
Baiyoke 2 Tower (in Pratunam)	1997	88 storeys (304 metres)
Maha Nakorn (in Sathorn)	To be completed in 2014	77 storeys (310 metres)

SHOPPING-BAG BABY SCANDAL
· · · · · · ·

A strange kidnapping case occurred in June 1980 when a desperate Danish couple kidnapped a baby girl and snuck her out of the country in a shopping bag. The Danish couple reportedly gave the baby's biological mother 4,700 baht for the infant, but Thai authorities turned the couple down when they tried to make the adoption legal. The couple then drugged the baby and smuggled her onto a plane. After the parents' arrest in Denmark, the 11-month-old baby Louise was returned to Thailand and given to legal adoptive parents. The story, which made headlines for months, did not end there. Weeks after the new parents received the baby, the adoptive father, a police captain, was murdered in an apparently unrelated event.

A GUIDE TO ROYAL TITLES
· · · · · · ·

The top five birth titles of royal descendants are:

1. **Chao fa** (full title: *somdet chao fa*). This title is conferred on the immediate children of the king and his queen or royal consort. It is equivalent to His/Her Royal Highness in English.

2. **Phra ong chao**. This title is conferred on the immediate children of the king and a non-royal concubine. It is also equivalent to His/Her Royal Highness in English.

3. **Mom chao**. This title is conferred on the sons and daughters of princes at the rank of *chao fa* or *phra ong chao*. They are the last generation who may be considered real princes or princesses. It is equivalent to His/Her Serene Highness in English.

4. **Mom rajawongse**. This title is conferred on the children of *mom chao* princes, and they are considered neither fully royal, nor of common status. There is no English equivalent of this title.

5. **Mom luang**. This title is conferred on the children of *mom rajawongse* males, and they are considered commoners. The children of male *mom luang* do not bear any royal titles but they may add "na Ayudhaya" to their surnames to indicate their royal descent.

NUMBER OF REGISTERED VEHICLES
· · · · · · ·

In 2010, there were 22,040,198 vehicles registered in Thailand under the Motor Vehicle Act B.E. 2522 and Land Transport Act B.E. 2522. Nearly 15,000,000 of these vehicles were motorcycles, and 6,444,531 of the vehicles were registered in Bangkok. As of 2011, 2,379,457 sedans were registered in Bangkok, accounting for more than half the total number nationwide.

Source: The Department of Land Transport, Ministry of Transport

POLITE SPEECH
· · · · · · ·

In order to express a level of politeness while speaking to others, short articles are used at the end of sentences.

Level of politeness	Male	Female
Very polite	*krap*	*ka*
Polite	*ha*	n/a
Casual	*na* and *ja*	*na* and *ja*
Impolite	*wa*	*wa*

NATIONAL SYMBOLS
· · · · · · ·

National animal	National architecture	National flower
Asian elephant	Sala Thai	Ratchaphruek
(*Elephas maximas*)	(Thai pavilion)	(*Cassia fistula linn*)

TOP 10 LOCAL FILM BLOCKBUSTERS OF ALL-TIME
· · · · · · ·

The list is dominated by *Mom Chao* Chatrichalerm Yukol's historical, royal epics, which typically garner tremendous media coverage and public support. In addition to being the biggest earner at the local box office, *The Legend of Suriyothai* is believed to have had the largest budget of any Thai production.

1. *The Legend of Suriyothai* (2001); directed by *Mom Chao* Chatrichalerm Yukol – 550 million baht
2. *The Legend of King Naresuan Part I* (2007); directed by *Mom Chao* Chatrichalerm Yukol – 237 million baht
3. *The Legend of King Naresuan Part II* (2007); directed by *Mom Chao* Chatrichalerm Yukol – 235 million baht
4. *The Legend of King Naresuan Part III* (2011); directed by *Mom Chao* Chatrichalerm Yukol – 204 million baht
5. *Tom Yum Goong* (2005); directed by Prachya Pinkaew – 183 million baht
6. *Bang Rajan* (2001); directed by Tanit Jitnukul – 151 million baht
7. *Nang Nak* (1999); directed by Nonzee Nimitbutr – 150 million baht
8. *The Holy Man* (*Luang Phi Teng*; 2005); directed by Note Chern Yim – 142 million baht
9. *Bangkok Traffic Love Story* (*Rod Faifa Mahanater*; 2009); directed by Adisorn Trisirikasem – 139 million baht
10. *My Girl* (*Fan Chan*; 2003); directed by 365 Film – 137 million baht

THE MANY MEANINGS OF MALAI
· · · · · · ·

A *malai* is the most common type of floral decoration or offering in Thailand. A *malai* is typically made from jasmine buds and common flowers such as roses, orchids or champak, and it can be bought from street vendors at markets and major intersections in Bangkok. As *malai* are handmade, prices depend on complexity.

Children offer *malai* to their parents, and students to their teachers, as a mark of respect. The offering can also be given to a guest who has just arrived or one that is departing as a sign of appreciation or to wish them good luck.

A *malai* is also presented together with lit candles and incense sticks to Buddha statues or images. Taxi and truck drivers place *malai* at the front of their cars to pay respect to guardian spirits.

Long *malai* with two ends are part of auspicious occasions such as weddings where they are given to the bride and groom to wear around their necks as a symbol of the eternal bond of matrimony.

BANGKOK'S SMALL GREEN LUNGS
· · · · · · ·

Bangkok has 2,582 public parks, covering a total area of 11,859 *rai* (1 *rai* equals 1,600 square metres). This works out to an average of 3.3 square metres of parkland per person (if using Bangkok's official population, which is much lower than the actual population). The World Health Organisation advises cities to offer a minimum of 9 square metres per person.

Sources: Bangkok Metropolitan Authority (BMA), World Health Organisation (WHO)

THE CORRUPTION SCALE
· · · · · · ·

Political and Economic Risk Consultancy (PERC) rated Thailand as the eleventh most corrupt country among 16 Asia-Pacific nations. On its scale, which ranges from 0-10, Thailand received a 7.55. The highest score (9.27) belonged to Cambodia, while Singapore had the lowest score (0.37).

Source: Political and Economic Risk Consultancy (PERC)

THE MYSTERY OF B.N.E.
· · · · · · ·

In 2009, three initials began to appear all over Bangkok's streets. Wherever you looked, B.N.E. was there, posted via stickers on phone boxes and streetlights, scrawled in marker on signs, and spray-painted in huge letters on walls. But B.N.E. wasn't just in Bangkok. The graffiti—especially the stickers—was seen all over the world, leading many to speculate it was the work of more than one person. In 2009, however, B.N.E. had an exhibition in New York City and was featured, though not identified, in a piece in *The New York Times*. Some tidbits about B.N.E., both the tag and the man, from the article:

- Said to be in his early 30s
- Believed to hail from New York City
- The meaning of the initials B.N.E. has never been divulged. "Breaking and Entering", "Bomb Nuclear Explosion", the author's initials? No one knows.
- New York, San Francisco, Prague, Hong Kong, Kuala Lumpur and Bangkok are among the cities that were blanketed by B.N.E. graffiti
- The graffiti artist goes through up to 10,000 stickers a month
- The initials are printed in Helevetica Neue Condensed font
- The graffiti artist has never been arrested. He says only a handful of people close to him know it is his handiwork.

A HOTEL INSTEAD OF A BROTHEL
· · · · · · ·

The following article appeared in the *Bangkok Post* in the 1960s:

"The Cabinet has approved a Department of Public Welfare plan to build a rehabilitation hotel for prostitutes.

One million baht will be allotted for the purpose, and thereafter 300,000 baht a year. The hotel will be able to house 100 women who are desirous of giving up their profession.

Besides having a place of shelter during their period of breaking away from a career of prostitution and seeking other types of employment, the women will be taught a respectable way of making a living and will be given help in improving their moral outlook.

If any prostitutes who are arrested by police refuse to go to the hotel, they will be sent to Koh Kled settlement, although later, if they are willing, they may be sent to the hotel for rehabilitation."

CACOPHONY OF EXCLAMATIONS
• • • • • •

These exclamations can be used in the following situations. It's best to ask a fluent Thai speaker for the exact pronunciation, tone and emotional import.

frightened .... *wui! wai! mhae! tai jing!*
surprised .... *hue! ha! o-ho!*
to acknowledge .... *aoe, aor* or *aor* (with high pitch)
hurt .... *oy oy! oui!*
feel sorry, sympathise .... *thoe, thoe* (with high pitch) or *phut thoe*
shout for someone .... *hoei! hey! ni!*
relieved .... *hoe* or *hoe* (with high pitch)
angry .... *mhae! chi cha!*

WAXING LYRICAL ABOUT THE DURIAN
• • • • • •

"... like eating a sweet raspberry blancmange in a lavatory."

—Anthony Burgess, *Time for a Tiger*

"Sweet, citrusy Silly Putty mixed with onion powder, marinated in spoiled milk."

—Kate Klonick, *Esquire magazine*, July 2007

"A rich custard highly flavoured with almonds gives the best general idea of it, but there are occasional wafts of flavour that call to mind cream-cheese, onion-sauce, sherry-wine, and other incongruous dishes. Then there is a rich glutinous smoothness in the pulp which nothing else possesses, but which adds to its delicacy. It is neither acid nor sweet nor juicy; yet it wants neither of these qualities, for it is in itself perfect. It produces no nausea or other bad effect, and the more you eat of it the less you feel inclined to stop. In fact, to eat durians is a new sensation worth a voyage to the East to experience."

—Alfred Russel Wallace, 19th-century naturalist

"... completely rotten, mushy onions."

—Andrew Zimmer, food writer, dining critic and chef

"Its taste can only be described as...indescribable, something you will either love or despise... Your breath will smell as if you'd been French-kissing your dead grandmother."

—Anthony Bourdain, food critic, author, television host and chef

"... its odor is best described as pig [excrement], turpentine and onions, garnished with a gym sock. It can be smelled from yards away."

—Richard Sterling, travel and food writer

THE TRUMAN SHOW STARRING A PANDA
· · · · · · ·

There are many things the world wastes bandwidth on, and one of them happens to be a 24-hour-a-day broadcast of a panda called "Lin Ping". On True Visions cable network, you can watch every single movement of the famous Lin Ping, whether she is eating, sleeping or rolling around in her poop. Did we list sleeping yet? She was born in 2009 in Chiang Mai Zoo (her mother was artificially inseminated) and has been a local celebrity ever since. (Well, to her loyal fan club anyway.) While most people probably spend no more than three seconds on this channel, there are some die-hard fans who watch her every day for no less than half an hour and meet up every week with other fans to chat about the captive bear.

FOREIGN HUSBANDS
· · · · · · ·

Udon Thani province has the highest numbers of Thai women married to foreigners, with more than 20,000 couples. In one village in Nong Wua So district, there are estimated to be 2,800 incidences, although only 500 of these couples are registered in Thailand as married. The most common nationality of foreign husbands is German.

Source: Udon Thani's Office of the Ministry of Social Development and Human Security

PLAGUED BY PLASTIC
· · · · · · ·

The Thai population produces around 40,000 tonnes of garbage daily. On average, the population of Bangkok produces about 8,500 tonnes daily, 1,800 tonnes of which are plastic bags. If the use of plastic bags were eliminated, the city would save about 650 million baht a year (US$21 million) in garbage collection costs and also reduce its annual carbon dioxide production by one million tonnes.

Source: Green World Foundation and Pollution Control Department, Ministry of Natural Resources and Environment

SELECTED SNAKEBITE MARKS
. . . .

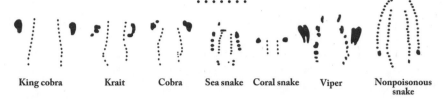

| King cobra | Krait | Cobra | Sea snake | Coral snake | Viper | Nonpoisonous snake |

FROM NONG TO YAI
. . . .

To create familiarity but also show respect, all Thais typically refer to each other in terms of familial relationships, such as calling an older colleague *pi* (meaning "older sister" or "older brother"). This rather hierarchical system can at first require an assessment of someone's age against one's own or that of your parents. Here are the most common usages:

Word	Actual meaning	Used to refer to someone that is …
nong	younger brother/sister	younger than you (both genders)
pi	older brother/sister	older than you (both genders)
pa	elder sister of the mother/father	older than your parents (female)
lung	elder brother of the mother/father	older than your parents (male)
na	younger brother/sister of the mother	younger than your parents but older than you (both genders)
ta	father of the mother	as old as your grandfather (male)
yai	mother of the mother	as old as your grandmother (female)

These words can be used alone or added before each individual's name. However, they need to be used carefully. Some people might feel uncomfortable to be called by a name that isn't actually appropriate for their age. But this system also may partially explain why Thais are not shy about asking about someone's age.

COMPUTER CRIME ACT
. . . .

Backed by Thailand's Computer Crime Act B.E. 2550 (2007), police blocked 60,000 URLs and more than 70 websites for content deemed detrimental to national security between 2008 to mid-2011.

THE WORLD'S LARGEST BUDDHA
· · · · · · ·

The largest Buddha statue in the world is called Phra Buddha Maha Navamintara Sakayamuni Sri Wisetchaichan and is located at Wat Muang in Wisetchaichan district, Angthong province. The Buddha statue is in *pang manvichai* posture, legs crossed with the right hand on right knee and left hand in the middle of the lap. The width from the right knee to the left one is 63.5 metres and the statue is 93 metres tall. Construction took 16 years (from 1991–2007) and cost 106,261,090 baht (approximately US$3.4 million).

Source: Wat Muang, Angthong province

THE PURE PLEASURE OF FISH SAUCE
· · · · · · ·

Thailand is the number one exporter in the world of this stinky condiment. Known in Thai as *nam pla*, the salty, fishy-smelling, thin sauce is used as a substitute for salt and is integral to many Thai dishes. *Nam pla* is made from fermented fish from the *Stolephorus* genus (such as *pla katak* and *pla saitan*) and comes in three types:

- Pure fish sauce, which is made from fermented fish or fish residue only
- Fish sauce from other marine life such as shrimp, squid, and shellfish, sometimes in combination with pure fish sauce
- Diluted fish sauce, which is pure fish sauce or fish sauce from other marine life mixed with non-hazardous substances such as artificial colours and fragrances

Pure fish sauce must:

- Have a fishy smell and taste accordingly
- Must be clear
- The salt content cannot be less than 200 grammes per litre
- The total nitrogen content cannot be less than 9 grammes per litre
- The amino acid nitrogen content should be between 40–60% of the total nitrogen content
- Glutamic acid content per total nitrogen is between 0.4–0.8
- No artificial colour, except caramel colour
- No artificial sweeteners except sugar

Fish sauce usually has a three-year shelf life prior to opening.

Source: Pichai Fish-Sauce Co, Ltd

POSTURES OF THE BUDDHA
· · · · · · ·

More than 70 postures have been made into statues to represent different activities and phases of the Buddha's life. There are seven postures of the Buddha corresponding to the different days of the week—the reason for an eighth posture, representing Wednesday night, is explained on page 34.

Day	Posture name	Position
Sunday	*Pang Tawai Netra*	Standing with both hands crossed in the middle of the lap (right hand on left hand), palms up, eyes open, and in a mindful state.
Monday	*Pang Hamsamut*	Standing with both hands raised next to the chest and palms facing forward.
Tuesday	*Pang Sai Yat* or *Parinippan*	Lying on the right side, both eyes closed, head on a pillow, right hand supports the head, left hand on left side of the body, left foot on right foot, with feet aligned.
Wednesday (day)	*Pang Aum Batr*	Standing and holding a bowl in his hands.
Wednesday (night)	*Pang Palilai*	Standing with hands on thighs and eyes closed. A monkey offers honeycomb while a small elephant offers a pot of water.
Thursday	*Pang Samati*	Sitting crossed-legged (right leg on left leg) with both hands on the lap (right hand on left hand).
Friday	*Pang Rampueng*	Standing with both hands crossed at the chest (right hand on left hand).
Saturday	*Pang Naga Prok*	Sitting crossed-legged (right leg on left leg), both hands on the lap like *Pang Samati*, with a five- or nine-headed Naga behind the head, or curled into a seat or around the Buddha's lower body.

VOTING TRIVIA
· · · · · · ·

- You must be 18 or older to vote.
- Monks, prisoners and mentally insane people are not eligible to vote.
- If you are a foreigner, you must have held Thai nationality for more than five years in order to be eligible to vote.
- If you damage, destroy or draw on campaign posters, the party can sue you, which could lead to one to 10 years in jail or a 20,000 to 200,000 baht fine.
- Taking a picture of your ballot card and posting it onto social media networks such as Facebook or Twitter can lead to a one-year jail term or a fine of up to 20,000 baht.
- Ripping up your own ballot card is also considered a crime. In recent years, several people who have ripped up their ballots as a form of political protest have been arrested.

Source: *Bangkok Post*

Sunday   Monday   Tuesday   Wednesday (day)

Wednesday (night)   Thursday   Friday   Saturday

COST OF LIVING IN BANGKOK AFTER WORLD WAR II (C. 1946)
· · · · · · ·

Black coffee	50 satang (equivalent to half of a baht)
Rice with curry	1 baht
Bowl of rice noodles	1 baht
Bull tongue stew at Silom Restaurant	10 baht
Pork chop at Silom Restaurant	10 baht
Four-page newspaper	50 satang
Axe	70 baht (up from 1 baht before the war)

Source: Nai Hon Huay, famous radio news anchor from Ubon Ratchathani, as reported on www.2bangkok.com

BUDDHIST PRECEPTS

· · · · · · ·

The vast majority of Thais are Buddhist. The five precepts of Buddhism state that one should abstain from:

- taking life
- obtaining something that was not given
- sexual misconduct
- lying
- drinking alcohol or consuming any intoxicating substances

Monks must uphold 227 precepts. Among the precepts are:

- To remain celibate
- Not to ejaculate, except while sleeping
- To abstain from any physical contact with women
- Not to act as matchmaker or mediator between male and female partners (not even with married couples)
- Not to keep robes that have not been used for more than ten days
- Not to take off one's robes (even for one night)
- Not to receive money and buy or sell anything with money
- Not to give one's robes to other monks and then ask for their return
- Not to swim for leisure
- Not to eat leftover food
- Robes must cover the knees and belly button
- Not to sleep in the same room for more than three nights with anyone who is not a monk or novice monk
- Not to dig soil or ask someone to dig
- Not to shower too often (only when necessary)
- Not to label their own robes
- Not to invite any women to act as a companion when travelling
- Not to accept an invitation to eat and then eat elsewhere
- Not to receive more than three bowls during an alms round
- Not to request more than given when invited to eat
- To only eat food that is given by another person

Source: National Office of Buddhism

CHINESE IMMIGRATION
. . . .

The Chinese have been migrating south to Siam for centuries. Waves of migration, often to escape hardship, have seen the Chinese population in Thailand increase from an estimated 230,000 in 1825 to 792,000 in 1910 to 8 million today (14% of the population). Among the estimated 8 million ethnic Chinese in Thailand, 56% are Teochew, 16% are Hakka, 11% are Hainanese, 7% are Hokkien, and 7% are Cantonese. The other 3% came from a range of other ethnic groups. As the Chinese are highly assimilated into Thai culture through intermarriage, they no longer form a distinct community living in a separate enclave as they do in many cities.

HEY YOU! FARANG!
. . . .

Farang is the commonly heard name used by Thais for people of European ancestry (or Caucasians). The term doesn't have derogative connotations. According to an account by the Thai historian Prince Damrong, this label came from the Persian word, *faranji* or *feringi*, a name that was used by the Thais in reference to the Portuguese, who were the first group of foreigners to visit Siam during the Ayudhya period. *Farang* also has another totally unrelated meaning, guava.

GARUDA: THE MOUNT OF VISHNU
. . . .

Hindus believe that a mythical half-bird, half-man creature called Garuda transported the God Vishnu wherever he went. The symbolism of Garuda has been associated with Siamese or Thai kingship as far back as the Ayudhya-period reign of King U Thong (mid-fourteenth century). He used a Garuda carved from ivory as his seal. The royal seal of the current monarch bears the Garuda as an imprint.

Today, the Thai government's stationery, uniforms and other important items bear an image of the Garuda as an indication of its loyalty and service to the king. The Garuda is also used as a royal insignia on other paraphernalia related to the palace.

Private corporations may be conferred with the seal of the Garuda in honour of their service to the country and monarchy. These companies and shops then erect and display a Garuda crest above their entrances.

RESTRICTIONS ON THE SALE OF ALCOHOL
· · · · · · ·

It is against Thai law to sell alcoholic beverages in the following places or situations:

- on Buddhist national holidays (*Makha Bucha, Visaka Bucha, Asalaha Bucha and Buddhist Lent*), except in hotels.
- from 6pm the night before a district or general election through midnight of the election day.
- in temples or on the premises of any religious institution.
- in hospitals, schools, or on the premises of any educational institution.
- in governmental offices, except in their clubs or shops.
- in petrol stations or shops on their premises.
- in public parks.
- in an automated machine, or through street vendors.
- to persons below the age of 20.
- to persons already intoxicated.
- outside the hours of 11pm to 2pm, and 5pm to midnight.

THE TALENTED TONY JAA
· · · · · · ·

Thai film actor and former stuntman Tony Jaa shot to international stardom when the action flicks *Ong Bak* and *Tom Yum Goong* became hits. Jaa's high-octane scenes were full of jaw-dropping stunts performed by Jaa himself and unaided by special effects. Here is some more Tony Jaa trivia:

- His birth name was Worawit Yeeram. When he started his career in entertainment, he changed it to Phanom Yeeram. His name now is Thatchakorn Yeeram. It is not uncommon for Thais to change their names.
- Tony Jaa is how he is known internationally. However, he is commonly known among Thais as Jaa Phanom.
- The nickname Jaa was given to him by his neighbours, not his parents.
- He incorporates many types of martial arts into his stunts, including *Muay Thai*, taekwando, *zui-quan* ("Chinese drunken fists"), kung fu, aikido, judo, karate, capoeira, Brazilian jiujitsu and mixed martial arts (MMA).
- He claims to have invented a new style of martial arts which he has named *nattayut*. It is a combination of traditional *khon* (Thai mask dancing), break-dancing and martial arts.

HOW TO IDENTIFY A WHITE ELEPHANT
· · · · · · ·

According to legend, Queen Maya, the Buddha's mother, dreamt of a white-coloured elephant entering her womb, and upon waking found herself with child—this son grew up to become the Buddha. As the elephant was also the powerful mount of the Hindu god Indra, it is not surprising that the animal is revered in predominantly Buddhist and Hindu nations. For centuries, the monarchs of these countries have collected "white" elephants to increase their prestige. Siam's flag, designed by Rama II, featured a white elephant as the nation's symbol until 1917.

White elephants are not actually white, but full or partially albino. Ideally, their skin colour should be light yellow, grey, red, purple or bluish, and the mouth's interior should resemble the pinkness of a lotus bud. White edges around the eyes, ears and trunk tip are especially admired. White toenails and a sprout of red hair are also prized. The testicles should be close to white in colour.

Anyone who finds an elephant with all or some of these characteristics is obliged to inform the authorities so that the elephant can be assessed by palace officials. The first white elephant sent to the current monarch, King Bhumibol, was found in 1956 and named Phra Savet Adulyadej Pahon. The king currently has in possession a number of white elephants. They are usually kept at Chitralada Villa in Bangkok, at the Sakon Nakhon stables, and at Klai Kungwon Palace in Hua Hin. Ten of the king's white elephants have royal ranks and have been through the Brahmin naming ceremony, in which it is dressed in ceremonial costume, has sacred water poured over it and is bestowed a name by the king, while traditional music is played.

COLOUR-CODED DAYS
· · · · · · ·

In Thailand, the days of the week are named after various gods and each day has a corresponding colour with which the day is linked. As Thais make a point of knowing on which day of the week they were born, they will often assume that particular day's colour as their own auspicious colour. Here are the different colours of the different days of the week:

Sunday	Red, for the sun god Phra Athit
Monday	Yellow, for the moon god Phra Chan
Tuesday	Pink, for the Mars god Phra Angkarn
Wednesday	Green, for the Mercury god Phra Phut
Thursday	Orange, for the Jupiter god Phra Paruhut
Friday	Blue, for the Venus god Phra Suk
Saturday	Purple, for the Saturn god Phra Sao

ROYAL BARGE PROCESSIONS
· · · · · · ·

R oyal progresses traditionally were made on land upon an open palanquin, and on water by barge. These processions were rare occasions in which the public could view the majesty of the king, and were thus accordingly grand. The former capital of Ayudhya was set amid a network of canals at the confluence of three rivers. Royal barges essentially constituted the ancient navy. King Maha Chakkraphat employed barges in wars against the Burmese, and installed cannon and animal figureheads on larger vessels. The main barges were used for ceremonial purposes, such as welcoming foreign officials. In recent times, the barge procession was used by King Bhumibol or royal representatives to travel down the Chao Phraya to present robes to senior monks to mark the start of the *kathin* season. Nowadays, the royal barge procession is a source of national pride and symbolism, and has been staged to mark significant anniversaries and events.

There are 52 barges operated by 2,082 men from the Royal Thai Navy. Among the key barges are:

- Anekchatbhunchonge royal barge: built during the reign of King Chulalongkorn
- Supannahongse royal barge: built during the reign of King Vajiravudh
- Anantanagaraj royal barge: built during the reign of King Vajiravudh
- Naraisongsuban royal barge: built during the reign of King Bhumibol in 1996 to celebrate the 50th anniversary of his accession to the throne

"YES! WE HAVE BANANAS!"
· · · · · · ·

klauy hom   *kluay kai*   *kluay hakmuk*

T he banana is one of the first fruits cultivated by man. Thailand is believed to be the origin of more than 13 species of bananas and the fruit, its skin and leaves are used for many different purposes. Today, there are more than 60 varieties of banana on the market. Some of the most popular varieties are *kluay kai, kluay tani, kluay namwa, kluay hakmuk,* and *klauy hom.* The most commonly exported type of banana is *kluay homtong* (Gros Michel).

ON "TRANSIENT WIVES"
* * * * * * *

"The Europeans that trade with Siam provide themselves as they will do in Pegou with transient wives and more or less on similar terms and no one would think it shameful to have as many transient husbands, but on the contrary to be an honour to have been loved by so many different men." –British Sea Captain Alexander Hamilton, 17th century

THE EFFECTS OF SOME FOODS ACCORDING TO CHINESE MEDICINE
* * * * * * *

Arrest bleeding .... black fungus, chestnut, chicken eggshell, cottonseed, cuttle bone, guava, lotus plumule, spinach, vinegar

Calming .... liquorice, lily flower

Reduce perspiration .... oyster shell, peach

Reduce urination .... raspberry

Reduce seminal ejaculation .... lotus plumule, oyster shell, walnut, black fungus

Disperse blood coagulation .... brown sugar, chive, chive root, crab, hawthorn fruit, saffron, vinegar

Eliminate sputum .... Chinese wax gourd, clam, longevity fruit, pear, radish, sea grass, seaweed

Promote milk secretion .... common carp, lettuce

Lubricate intestines .... apricot seed (bitter and sweet), banana, cow's milk, soybean oil, peach, walnut, watermelon

Promote urination .... asparagus, barley, Chinese cabbage, Chinese wax gourd, coffee, corn, corn silk, cucumber, grape, hops, Job's tears, kidney bean

Sharpen vision .... abalone, bitter gourd, wild cucumber, freshwater clam, cuttlefish

Strengthen the heart .... coffee, wheat

Strengthen the kidneys .... black sesame seed, string bean, sword bean, wheat, kidneys

Strengthen the spleen .... beef, gold carp, ham, horse bean, hyacinth bean, polished rice, Job's tears

Relieve hot sensations .... chicken egg white, crab, mung bean

Source: *Chinese System of Food Cures* by Henry C. Lu, 1986

HOW TO ARTIFICIALLY INSEMINATE AN ASIAN ELEPHANT
· · · · · · ·

1. Monitor the female elephant's oestrus cycle—each cycle lasts four months—and identify the specific hormone surge that causes ovulation.

2. Collect semen from the male elephant 12 to 24 hours before the insemination procedure is due to begin.

3. Bathe the female in warm, soapy water, and then give a warm water enema to cleanse the rectum.

4. Place the female under ultrasound to visualise its reproductive tract.

5. Guide a catheter through the tract, and deposit semen directly into the cervix or uterus.

DEAD MAN WALKING
· · · · · · ·

The most severe punishment allowed under law in Thailand is the death sentence, which has existed since the Ayudhya period centuries ago.

In the oldest existing record of Thai legislation, *The Three Seals Code* (1805), 21 techniques of execution are listed. These methods typically involved a long process of torture, including stripping the skin, hooking the lip to a gaff, being burned alive or showered with boiling oil, being eaten by wild dogs, clubbing with a bludgeon, and whipping using a rattan with spikes. It is believed however that these methods were recorded in law to frighten and deter people from committing crimes, and were not commonly practised.

The Three Seals Code remained in court use till 1908 when, during the reign of King Chulalongkorn, the laws were modified and the various execution methods were changed to decapitation. The shift from absolute to constitutional monarchy in 1932 also brought about a change in the method of execution. From 1934 to 2006, 323 convicts were executed by gunshot. Thereafter, the Thai government changed the official method of execution to lethal injection.

Crimes punishable with the death sentence include:

- Arson
- Crimes against His Majesty the King and Her Majesty the Queen, the heir apparent, and the regent
- Crimes against other nations' head of state
- Crimes related to "Type 1" drugs such as heroin
- Kidnapping
- Premeditated murder, and murder to conceal rape, sexual assault or robbery
- Terrorism
- Treason

ON OPIUM
· · · · · · ·

- Opium grows best in the highlands at altitudes between 1,000 to 2,000 metres.
- To create raw opium, the seed pod is sliced to release its white and milky juice which will turn brown and sticky when dried. It can be kept in this form for years without losing its potency.
- Before it can be smoked, raw opium must be boiled first.
- While opium plantations are currently illegal, they still can be found in remote areas of Chiang Rai, Mae Hong Son and Tak provinces.
- In order to trick law enforcement or government officials, opium is typically planted with other crops or in a way that imitates the appearance of other legal crops.
- Opium is used as a base substance in the production of morphine, heroin and codeine.

POPULATION TRENDS
· · · · · · ·

Thailand is the 20th most populous country in the world, with an estimated population of just over 67 million people. Both the population and life expectancy have risen steadily over the last seven decades.

Year	Population	Life expectancy (male/female)
1950	18,662,000	49/51
1960	26,257,916	54/59
1970	34,397,374	58/61
1980	44,824,540	61/65
1990	54,548,530	66/71
2000	60,916,441	70/75
2010	65,479,453	70/76

NO CHOPSTICKS: THAI EATING ETIQUETTE
· · · · · · ·

- Use a fork and spoon (a spoon to put the food into your mouth and a fork to help navigate the food onto the spoon).
- Sometimes food may be served as an individual meal but Thais usually eat communally with all the dishes in the middle of the table and share all the courses.
- Use a separate spoon for each dish that is shared. A small bowl can be used for your soup. If there is no small bowl available, use a separate spoon to place the soup onto your spoon.
- When chewing, the lips should be closed tight, no chewing sounds, do not talk while food is in your mouth, and do not open your mouth while there is food still inside. That's right— shut your mouth.
- If it is necessary to spit something out, spit it on your spoon first and then put it on the edge of the plate.
- To indicate when you are finished eating, put the fork and spoon together and lay them in the middle of the plate at twelve o'clock.

A CULTURE OF CHEATING?
· · · · · · ·

The 2012 global sex survey conducted by condom manufacturer Durex (of 29,000 people worldwide) found that Thai men ranked number one in the world for cheating on their girlfriends or wives, while Thai women ranked number two.

Fifty-four percent of Thai men surveyed admit to having cheated on their girlfriends or wives (South Korean men placed second at 34%), while 59% of Thai women admitted to cheating, second only to Ghanaian women at 62%.

Source: Durex Sexual Wellbeing Global Survey 2012

THAI WORKERS ABROAD
· · · · · · ·

The top five countries by number of registered Thai workers:

Taiwan	40,927
Singapore	12,179
South Korea	10,094
United Arab Emirates	8,308
Israel	8,136

Source: Department of Employment, Ministry of Labour (updated as of 2010)

FULL MOON PARTY
. . . .

Many young adults travelling to Thailand are drawn to the island of Phangan in Surat Thani province because of its massive full moon party at Haad Rin. The seaside music rave brings in between 20,000 to 30,000 tourists each full moon, providing a great source of income for the locals.

The inaugural full moon party in 1985 was simple compared to the wild spectacle it is today. Back then, the island had no electricity and restricted road access, and Haad Rin was a serene beach with white sand and crystal clear water. The party that took place on the night of a full moon had been meant as a gesture of thanks to 20 to 30 travellers who were staying there.

As with most large outdoor events, full moon partygoers are sometimes injured. The most common injuries are cuts on the feet as many people go barefoot on the beach and are unable to see clearly in the dark. Some partygoers have drowned after falling asleep on the beach, so drunk that they were oblivious to the incoming tide. Mainland hospitals in Surat Thani province also brace every month for an influx of visits.

MISS THAILAND
. . . .

- The beauty pageant first started with only nine contestants as part of the Constitution Fair in 1934.
- It was initially called Miss Siam and changed to Miss Thailand in 1939 when the country's name was changed.
- The first swimsuit contest was held in 1950.
- The contest was originally managed by the Interior Ministry.
- Since 1934, there have been 44 Miss Siam/Miss Thailand winners.
- From 1965 to 1999, the winner of Miss Thailand represented the country in the Miss Universe competition. In 2000, the organiser lost the license, and another organiser formed Miss Thailand Universe. Following yet another change in management, the title Miss Thailand Universe was changed to Miss Universe Thailand in 2012.
- In 1985, the Miss Thailand World contest was formed. The winner of the title Miss Thailand World represents Thailand in the Miss World contest.

Source: www.missthailand.mediathai.net

OLYMPIC HEROES
· · · · · · ·

Thailand first participated in the Olympic Games in 1952 when they were held in Helsinki, Finland. To date, Thailand's Olympic athletes have won 24 medals (seven golds, six silvers, and 11 bronzes). The first Olympic medal was awarded to Payao Poontarat, who won a bronze for boxing in 1976. Thailand's seven gold medals were won by:

Somluck Kumsing

- Somluck Kumsing in boxing (Atlanta, 1996)
- Wijan Ponlid in boxing (Sydney, 2000)
- Manus Boonjumnong in boxing (Athens, 2004)
- Udomporn Polsak in weightlifting (Athens, 2004)
- Pawina Thongsuk in weightlifting (Athens, 2004)
- Prapawadee Jaroenrattanatarakul in weightlifting (Beijing, 2008)
- Somjit Jongjorho in boxing (Beijing, 2008)

ORIGINAL LÈSE-MAJESTÉ LAW
· · · · · · ·

A Siamese proto law of *lèse-majesté* was included in *The Three Seals Code* (1805), a codification of laws from the Ayudhya period. Provision 7 of the Law on Revolt and Warfare prescribed the following by way of penalty: "Whosoever dares, without fear, to impudently speak of the king, disparages of royal acts, edicts or commands, that person has transgressed the royal criminal laws of the king and shall be punished with the punishment of Eight Instances, namely:

1. Beheading and seizure of household
2. Slitting the mouth and cutting off the ears, hands and feet
3. Given 25 or 30 lashes with a leather whip
4. Imprisoned for a month and then made to cut grass for elephants
5. Fined fourfold and made into a serf
6. Fined twice
7. Fined once
8. Pardoned from punishment on the promise of good behaviour."

Source: *King Bhumibol Adulyadej: A Life's Work*

GOVERNMENT SALARIES
• • • • • • •

Prime Minister or President of the Parliament...................................... 125,590 baht per month

Deputy Prime Minister .... 119,920 baht per month

Cabinet Minister, Vice President of the Parliament............................. 115,740 baht per month
or Head of the Opposition Party

Member of the House of Representatives .... 113,560 baht per month

Source: *Daily News* (8 August 2011); totals are a combination of the monthly salary plus monthly honorarium

A COLLECTION OF FIRSTS
• • • • • • •

1844 – Published by American missionary Dr Dan Beach Bradley in separate Thai and English editions, *Bangkok Recorder* was the first newspaper printed in Siam.

1864 – The first paved road, Charoen Krung (New Road), was completed.

1874 – A Chinese merchant opened the first pawn shop.

1875 – The first telegraph, which transmitted messages from Bangkok to Paknam (Samut Prakarn province) over a distance of 45 kilometres, was installed.

1881 – The Minister of Defense initiated the introduction of the first telephone connection between Bangkok and Paknam so that he could receive reports on the movement of ships.

1884 – Electricity was introduced, first at the Ministry of Defense, and then at the Grand Palace. It was introduced to the public in 1890.

1928 – The first lottery ticket was issued by the government.

1939 – The first school for the blind was opened by an American, Genevieve Caulfield, who was also blind. The school was also the first in Thailand aimed at disabled students.

1955 – The first television station, owned by Thai Television Company, started broadcasting as Channel 4.

1961 – The first National Economic Development Plan was initiated under the government of Field Marshal Sarit Thanarat. These plans became instrumental in Thailand's economic development over the second half of the 20th century.

1963 – Automatic traffic lights were introduced at 43 junctions in Bangkok.

1971 – The first university that did not require an entrance exam, Ramkamhaeng University ignited the expansion of educational opportunities in the country.

1975 – The first trade was completed at the Securities Exchange of Thailand (SET).

1981 – The first expressway, covering a distance of 27.1 kilometres, opened to traffic.

1983 – The nation's first ATM was installed by Siam Commercial Bank.

1986 – The first mobile phone was introduced by the Telephone Organisation of Thailand.

THE WORST DISASTERS
. . . .

Event	Year and province	Description
The worst fire	1993 – Bangkok	188 people were killed and several hundred more were injured in a fire at Kader Industrial factory. Factory workers could not escape because the emergency doors had always been locked to prevent theft.
The worst train crash	1979 – Bangkok	51 people died and 184 were injured when a freight train crashed into a passenger train in Taling Chan (west of Bangkok).
The worst road accident	1990 – Bangkok	A truck transporting flammable gas overturned, started leaking the gas and then exploded, burning 81 people to death on New Petchaburi Road.
The worst plane crash	1991 – Suphanburi	Engine failure on a Lauda Air Boeing 767 caused the plane to break apart mid-flight, killing all 223 passengers and crew.
The worst flood	2011 – Bangkok and another 64 provinces	Major floods covered more than half of the country and persisted for almost six months, causing 730 deaths and disrupting the lives of more than 13 million people.
The worst natural disaster	2004 – Ranong, Phang-nga, Phuket, Krabi, Trang and Satun	A 9.3-magnitude earthquake off the coast of Sumatra sent tsunami waves rushing over six provinces in southern Thailand, killing an estimated 8,212, with 5,395 officially confirmed dead.
The worst mudslide	1988 – Nakhon Si Thammarat and Surat Thani	A massive mudslide sent logs crashing down the mountains, killing 317 people.

THE AIDS EPIDEMIC
. . . .

In 1984, Thai doctors confirmed the first Thai HIV patient in Thailand. Since then, more than 1.1 million people have been diagnosed with HIV, and more than 600,000 have died of AIDS. As of 2009, according to UNICEF, there were 530,000 people living with HIV (1.9% of the adult population) in Thailand.

According to the Ministry of Public Health, among registered patients:

- Almost 25% were 30–34 years old
- 84% contracted the disease from sexual activities
- 7.8% do not recall their risk factors
- 4.4% contracted the disease from needles
- 3.6% were infected at birth
- 0.02% contracted the disease from a blood transfusion

ILLICIT FOOD FOR MONKS
· · · · · · ·

When a monk receives food from the public during his morning alms round, he must accept and consume what he is given, in whatever combination or form. However, according to guidelines offered by ancient Buddhist texts, lay people should not offer monks the following meats:

- Human flesh
- Elephant meat
- Horse meat
- Dog meat
- Snake meat

- Lion meat
- Bengal tiger meat
- Yellow tiger meat
- Leopard meat
- Bear meat

STRICT DRESS CODES FOR STUDENTS
· · · · · · ·

Thai students in public schools are required to adhere to the regulations for standard attire. The public school uniform for female students is typically a white short-sleeved blouse and navy blue skirt, although a handful of schools permit black skirts. Boys are obliged to wear white short-sleeved shirts and black, navy blue or khaki shorts. Here is an example of the strict regulations in attire for a male student at one public school:

- Shirts should be white but non-translucent, with elbow-length sleeves, white buttons 1 cm in diameter, a left chest pocket, and without a pleat at the back. The shirt should be tucked in at all times.
- Shorts should be black and reach no more than 5 cm above the knees, with two front pleats, 5 to 7 belt loops, and pockets on either side but not at the back.
- Belts should be black and 3–4 cm wide, with a rectangular buckle and one loop.
- Shoes should be black trainers with smooth-surfaced soles, and without patterns and white rims.
- Socks should be white and not too thick. When folded down, the top of the socks should not reach higher than the middle of the shin.
- Hair should be cut as close as possible to the skin. Side partings should not be longer than 4 cm. Shaved heads, sideburns, beards, dyed or permed hair, and the use of any kind of hair product, are prohibited.

ROYAL ANTHEM VERSUS NATIONAL ANTHEM
· · · · · · ·

In 1871, a young King Chulalongkorn visited the British colony of Singapore and heard "God Save the Queen" during a welcoming ceremony. On the same trip, in the Dutch East Indies (later Indonesia), the king was asked what music should herald his arrival and realised there was none. Soon after, King Chulalongkorn commissioned the composition of the royal anthem, eventually settling on a tune created by Russian composer Pyotr Schurovsky, with lyrics by Prince Narisara Nuvadtivongs (later modified by King Vajiravudh). This anthem is still played at official occasions, royal birthdays, and at ceremonies at which the monarch, the queen, the crown prince, or their royal representatives are present. It is also played before the beginning of major public entertainment and sporting events as well as before the screening of films. Everyone must stand when it is played. The anthem is written in the centuries-old language of *rajasap* so a literal translation is essentially impossible.

Thailand also has a national anthem, which was created in 1932 following the end of absolute monarchy. It was composed by German composer, Peter Feit, with lyrics by Khun Wichitmatra. In 1939, when the country's name was changed from Siam to Thailand, the lyrics were modified by Luang Saranuprabhandi. The national anthem is broadcast on national television and radio everyday at 8am and 6pm. It is also played in schools and public institutions. Like the royal anthem, everyone must stand when it is played.

THE TEN LONGEST RIVERS IN THAILAND
· · · · · · ·

1. Chi river: from Phetchabun province to Ubon Ratchathani province – 765 kilometres
2. Nan river: from Nan province to Nakhon Sawan province – 740 kilometres
3. Ping river: from Chiang Mai province to Nakhon Sawan province – 715 kilometres
4. Mun river: from Nakhon Ratchasima province to Udon Thani province – 614 kilometres
5. Yom river: from Payao province to Nakhon Sawan province – 555 kilometres
6. Pasak river: from Loei province to Ayutthaya province – 510 kilometres
7. Songkram river: Sakon Nakhon province to Nakhon Phanom province – 420 kilometres
8. Kwai Yai river: from Tak province to Kanchanaburi province – 380 kilometres
9. Chao Phraya river: from Nakhon Sawan province to Samut Prakan province – 370 kilometres
10. Wang river: from Chiang Rai province to Tak province – 335 kilometres

The Royal Anthem

We, subjects to His Great Majesty
Prostrate heart and head
To respect a king
Whose merits are boundless.
Sole and supreme sovereign,
Siam's greatest,
Foremost in honour,
We are joyous because of his rule.
The fruits of his wisdom preserve
The people in happiness and peace.
May it be that
Whatever he wills shall be done
According to the hopes of his great heart
As we wish him victory. Hurrah!

The National Anthem

Thailand unites all Thai people,
Every part of Thailand belongs to the Thai people.
Our country forever maintains its sovereignty,
Because the Thais have always been united.
Thai people are peace-loving,
But do not shrink from fighting.
Nor shall they suffer tyranny.
Thai people are ready to sacrifice every drop of blood for the nation
And its victories. Hurrah!

Source: There are no official translations. These are from the book *King Bhumibol Adulyadej: A Life's Work.*

QUOTABLES FROM THAKSIN SHINAWATRA
• • • • • •

The controversial former prime minister was known to make bold promises and speak off the cuff. Here are some quotes that made headlines:

"I will solve traffic problems in Bangkok within six months." – 1995

"If I were not a public figure, I wouldn't fly with THAI." – 2001

"The UN is not my father." – 2003

"I came here as a prime minister but left as an unemployed man." – 2006

"I will protect democracy with my life." – 2006

AMAZING TOURISM
. . . .

In 2011, 19,098,323 "tourists" entered Thailand, almost 20% more than the previous year. This number includes those who may have been visiting only for a day, to work or trade, from a neighbouring country. Here are the top 10 visitors by country:

1. Malaysia (2.47 million)
2. China (1.76 million)
3. Japan (1.12 million)
4. Russia (1,014,493)
5. South Korea (1,014,292)
6. India (916,787)
7. Laos (887,677)
8. Australia (854,064)
9. Great Britain (844,224)
10. United States (684,073)

Source: Tourism Authority of Thailand, Ministry of Tourism and Sports

EIGHTH DAY OF THE WEEK: MEET PHRA RAHU
. . . .

When Thais visit a temple, they will usually make an offering to the Buddha posture that corresponds to the day of the week on which they were born. But then why are there eight postures, not seven? Meet Phra Rahu, the god of eclipses, who is known for swallowing the sun and the moon, explaining a phenomenon that must have mystified the ancients. The Buddhist and Hindu cosmology offered Phra Rahu as a counterpoint to good, a god who plunged the world into chaos. His colour is black and his "day" is Wednesday night. Worshippers typically offer him black items, among them black candles, black flowers, black rice, black pudding and even Coca-Cola. To seek Phra Rahu's blessing is seen as a way to ward off bad luck, not invite trouble.

WASHING AWAY YOUR SINS
. . . .

The *Loy Krathong* festival typically occurs on the full moon night in November. *Loy Krathong* sees millions of people create or buy *krathong*, decorate them with flowers, incense sticks, and candles, and then head to a river or lake (or a bathtub if they are too far away) to float them. The original *krathong* was made from folded banana leaves to resemble the shape of an open lotus blossom. This offering to the Ganga (goddess of the river) is to express thankfulness and also ask for forgiveness, if people have exploited the river. The act of floating one's *krathong* down the river is also seen as a way to be purified of one's sins and start afresh. *Krathong* are made not only from banana leaves but other materials, including those seen as environmentally friendly, such as bread, which can be consumed by the freshwater fish.

CHITRALADA CLOTHING RESTRICTIONS
· · · · · · ·

Some parts of Chitralada Villa, which is His Majesty the King's current official royal residence, are open to the public. On the Villa's grounds are a school, health clinic, a dairy, a rice mill, as well as small plots on which crops are grown. However, in order to enter the premises, there are some clothing restrictions.

- One's shirt must be tucked in and the sleeves cannot be rolled up.
- Women have to wear skirts. A sarong is not permitted unless it is part of a national costume.
- You cannot wear only black or only black and white, as this is the typical dress code for funerals.
- T-shirts, sleeveless shirts, jeans and shorts are not allowed (unless it is part of a school uniform).
- Flip-flops or sandals cannot be worn (except by monks and novice monks).

A VERY LIGHT SNACK
· · · · · · ·

At least 194 insects in Thailand are edible, and indeed many are consumed as snacks, especially among people in the countryside. High in protein, the insects are prepared in a variety of different methods: grilled, deep-fried, stir-fried and boiled. Some of the insects contain extremely high levels of histamine, and thus consumption by those with allergies and asthma can cause death. House crickets have the highest level of cholesterol. In Bangkok, street vendors sell the insects not only to locals but also to adventurous tourists. A public health ministry report stated that more than two tonnes of insects are consumed each year and indicated that the eight most popular are:

Scorpion

House cricket

- House crickets
- Big-head crickets
- Silkworms
- Japanese grasshoppers
- Caterpillar wasps
- Scarab beetles
- Scorpions
- Bamboo worms

Bamboo worms

Scarab beetle

SOME MAJOR FOREIGN FILMS SHOT IN THAILAND
• • • • • • •

Title	Featuring	Location
Chang (1927)	Local amateur actors and wildlife, including a royal elephant	Nan
The Ugly American (1963)	Marlon Brando and Kukrit Pramoj	Bangkok
The Big Boss (1971)	Bruce Lee	Pak Chong, Nakhon Ratchasima
Duel Fists (1971)	Ti Lung	Bangkok
The Man with the Golden Gun (1974)	Roger Moore, Christopher Lee, Britt Ekland	Bangkok, Phang-nga Bay
The Deer Hunter (1978)	Robert DeNiro, Christopher Walken, Meryl Streep	Bangkok, Kanchanaburi
The Killing Fields (1984)	Sam Waterston, Haing S. Ngor, John Malkovich	Bangkok, Phuket, Cha-am, Hua Hin
Rambo III (1987)	Sylvester Stallone	Chiang Mai
Good Morning, Vietnam (1987)	Robin Williams	Phuket
Casualties of War (1989)	Michael J. Fox, Sean Penn	Phuket
Air America (1990)	Mel Gibson, Robert Downey Jr, Nancy Travis	Mae Hong Son
Operation Dumbo Drop (1995)	Danny Glover, Ray Liotta, Denis Leary	Mae Hong Son
Tomorrow Never Dies (1997)	Pierce Brosnan, Michelle Yeoh	Bangkok, Phang-nga Bay
The Beach (2000)	Leonardo DiCaprio	Koh Phi Phi, Krabi
In the Mood for Love (2000)	Maggie Chueng, Tony Leung	Bangkok
2046 (2004)	Tony Leung, Gong Li, Faye Wong	Bangkok
Alexander (2004)	Angelina Jolie, Colin Farell, Val Kilmer	Ubon Ratchathani, Saraburi
Around the World in Eighty Days (2004)	Jackie Chan, Steve Coogan	Krabi
American Gangster (2007)	Denzel Washington, Russell Crowe	Chiang Mai
Rambo (2008)	Sylvester Stallone	Chiang Mai
The Hangover Part II (2011)	Bradley Cooper, Zach Galifianakis, Ed Helms	Bangkok, Krabi

Marlon Brando and Kukrit Pramoj

Source: Thailand Film Office, Department of Tourism

"IT'S A BIRD, IT'S A PLANE, IT'S A - OH NO!"
· · · · · · ·

Dr Surasak Muangsombat is an expert in penis reattachment in Thailand. Since his first case in 1978, he and his team have reattached more than 33 penises, which were cut off by the victims' girlfriend or wife. In such situations, time is of the essence. If the penis can be reattached quickly, then it may function again. However, some perpetrators have made sure that would be impossible by flushing the penis down the toilet, tying it to a helium balloon, or via the most infamous method, feeding it to a duck. This latter method made such big news, "to cut and feed to the duck" (*that hai pet kin*) has become a common idiom when a Thai woman wants to express some menace towards her man.

FIVE MOST DESIRABLE COMPANIES TO WORK FOR
· · · · · · ·

According to a *Positioning* magazine survey of 569 people who were between the ages of 23–50 and already holding a job, the following companies were the most attractive employers:

1. PTT Public Co, Ltd
2. Siam Cement Group
3. Thai Airways International
4. Workpoint Entertainment
5. Toyota Motors Thailand

KRATOM COCKTAILS
· · · · · · ·

For centuries, farmers and rubber tappers who chewed the leaves of *kratom*, a common type of jungle tree, found they could work longer hours under the tropical sun. Others used it to stem diarrhoea. In recent times, however, teenagers in the three provinces of Thailand's Deep South (and now across the south) have turned to the leaf for pleasure, getting high from the cocktail mix of boiled *kratom*, cough syrup (one with codeine), Coca-Cola, ice, and occasionally either coffee, yogurt or even mosquito repellent. A survey of 1,000 teenagers conducted for Thailand's Office of the Narcotics Control Board found that 94% of teenagers in the region abused this non-alcoholic cocktail commonly called "4 x 100".

Sources: Department of Medical Services, Ministry of Public Health, *International Herald Tribune*

SOME THAI WORLD RECORDS
· · · · · · ·

The most expensive pet wedding (1996)
Until this year, the wedding of two rare diamond-eyed cats, Phet and Ploy, which cost over 400,000 baht, was the record-holder (a July 2012 dog wedding bested it). Five hundred guests attended, donating cash gifts of more than 1.5 million baht. The bride came in a Rolls Royce while the groom arrived in a helicopter. The best man was a parrot and an iguana was the maid of honour. No, we are not making this up.

Operation with the most veterinary surgeons (1999)
At Hang Chat Elephant Hospital in Lampang province, 30 veterinarians operated on an elephant which had stepped on a land mine. The elephant lost the lower part of its leg but was eventually fitted with a prosthetic.

The largest *tom yum kung* (1999)
Five thousands litres of *tom yum kung* soup was prepared by 12 chefs to promote Thai cuisine and the shrimp farming industry.

The largest motorcycle parade (2009)
The largest parade of automatic motorcycles took place in Nakhon Nayok province when 2,474 Yamaha Finos were used in a five-kilometre parade.

The scorpion woman (2009)
Kanchana Ketkaew broke her own endurance record by living with 5,000 scorpions in a glass box for 33 days.

ROAD WARRIORS
· · · · · · ·

" **T**he strength of the Thais' belief in their talismans is reflected in their expressionistic driving styles. Their seemingly total disregard of street signs, traffic lights, lanes and other motorists can of course be viewed two different ways: the Western way, irresponsible and negligent with an almost blatant disregard for human life, or the Thai way, as sort of subconscious poetic blend of technology and karma on wheels at high speed where only the dead deserve to die."
—Philip Blenkinsop, *The Cars That Ate Bangkok*

THE MORNING COMMUTE IN BANGKOK
• • • • • • •

The average walking speed of a human is around 5–6 km per hour, and the average running speed is twice that. But what about car traffic on the major roads in Bangkok?

Road	Average speed on weekdays, 6am–9am (km per hour)
Mahaisawan – Charoen Krung	12
Petchkasem – Charunsanitwong	12.4
Sathorn – Krung Thonburi	12.8
Taksin – Rama II	13.4
Ladprao	13.5
Baromrachonnee – Ratdamnoen Klang	15.0
Ramkamhaeng – Rama IX	16.1
Rama IV	16.6
Sukhumvit – Rama I	17.4
Prachachuen – Rama V	17.6
Phonyothin – Phyathai	18.1
Srinakarindra – Petchburi	20.3
Sirindhorn – Rajvithi	24.5
Vibhavadi Rangsit	39.7

Source: Office of Transport and Traffic Policy and Planning, Ministry of Transport

WHEN FAST-FOOD CHAINS FIRST OPENED IN THAILAND
• • • • • • •

1964 – Wimpy, opposite Thai-Daimaru mall in Bangkok
1980 – Pizza Hut in Pattaya
1984 – Kentucky Fried Chicken (KFC) in Central Ladprao, Bangkok
1984 – Dairy Queen in Robinson Silom, Bangkok
1985 – McDonald's in Sogo Department Store, Amarin Plaza, Bangkok
1990 – Arby's in Welco Supermarket, Pinklao and Central Ladprao, Bangkok
1990 – Burger King in Siam Square, Bangkok
1993 – Wendy's in The Mall, Thonburi
2003 – Subway in Silom, Bangkok

CHILDREN'S DAY SLOGANS

• • • • • • •

Since 1956, the prime minister has created a slogan in honour of Children's Day each year. Here are some examples:

Year	Slogan	Translation
1956	*chong bampen ton hai pen prayot tor suanruam*	Please behave in a useful way for the public good.
1960	*kor hai dek samai patiwat kong kapachao chong pen dek ti rak kwam sa-ard*	Wishing for the children of my revolutionary era to love hygeine.
1970	*dek prapruet di lae sueksa di tam hai mi anakot chamsai*	Children with good behaviour and possessing a good education will have a bright future.
1990	*otton kayan prayat pen kunna sombat kong dek thai*	The qualities of Thai children are perseverance, diligence and thriftiness.
2000	*mi winai fai rienru ku kunnatham nam prachathippatai*	Have discipline, seek knowledge, uphold virtue and lead democracy.
2010	*kit sangsan kayan rienru cherdchu kunnatham*	Think creatively, be diligent in seeking knowledge and uphold virtue.
2012	*samakki mi kwamru ku panya kong raksa kwam pen thai saijai technology*	Be united, have knowledge and wisdom, preserve "Thainess", and keep abreast of technology.

EIGHT THEORIES ABOUT JIM THOMPSON'S DISAPPEARANCE

• • • • • • •

Jim Thompson, a former US intelligence officer who later became a famous Thai silk entrepreneur, disappeared on 26 March 1967 while holidaying in the Cameron Highlands in Malaysia. A search ensued, with psychics, traditional Malaysian magicians and mediums joining. Although the mystery of his disappearance has never been solved, there have been many theories offered to explain what happened to him, among them:

- He fell down a ravine while walking in the jungle.
- Wild animals attacked him.
- He was kidnapped (by communists or the CIA).
- He fell into an aboriginal animal trap and was buried by tribesmen.
- He was run over by a truck and the driver disposed of his body.
- He was murdered during a botched robbery attempt.
- He staged his own disappearance.
- He committed suicide.

FARM LANGUAGE
• • • • • • •

Thais verbalise animal sounds a little differently from the rest of the world.

Birds	*jip jip*	Geckos	*tuk kae tuk kae*
Cats	*miaw miaw*	Goats	*bae bae*
Cows	*mor mor*	Frogs	*ob ob*
Crows	*ka ka*	Monkeys	*jiak jiak*
Dogs	*hong hong*	Pigs	*aut aut*
Ducks	*gaap gaap*	Roosters	*ek ei ek ek*
Elephants	*praen praen*	Bullfrogs	*aueng ang aueng ang*

PHRA VIHARN TEMPLE DISPUTE
• • • • • • •

The 11th-century Hindu temple Phra Viharn, which overlooks both Thailand and Cambodia from a dramatic cliff-top location, has been at the heart of an ownership and border dispute for decades. The Khmer-built temple, which can only be properly accessed from Si Saket province in northeastern Thailand, has been periodically closed to visitors during times of heated disagreement.

1904 – Siam officials and the French colonials ruling Cambodia agree to draw a border demarcating their territories. An agreement was made to use the Dângrêk Mountain Range as a watershed and border, which would have placed the temple in Thailand.

1907 – Having completed the survey work, French officials present a map with a border that detours from the watershed and places the temple in Cambodia. Thai officials do not dispute the border and circulate the map.

1954 – Following the withdrawal of French troops from Cambodia, Thai forces occupy the temple and the dispute over the temple's ownership becomes a contentious issue for years.

1958 – The two nations suspend diplomatic relations over the dispute.

1959 – The nations re-establish diplomatic relations and agree to let the International Court of Justice settle the argument.

1962 – The International Court of Justice rules by a 7-2 vote that the temple belongs to Cambodia. Thailand fumes and protests are staged, but the government ultimately agrees to respect the decision and hands over ownership to Cambodia.

2008 – After an application is submitted by Cambodia, UNESCO agrees to list the temple as a World Heritage site, over the protests of Thailand. Military clashes break out by the temple in October.

2011 – The temple is officially named a UNESCO World Heritage site.

THE LONE WINTER OLYMPIAN
* * * * * * *

P rawat Nagvajara, a 43-year-old Thai professor residing in Pennsylvania at the time, took part in the 2002 Winter Olympics in Salt Lake City, Utah, as the only representative of Thailand and the country's first-ever participant in the Winter Games. Prawat originally participated in the 30 km cross-country skiing race, but was disqualified after being lapped. He then finished 68th out of 71 racers in the 1.5 km sprint. In 2006, he again represented Thailand. He first saw snow when he was 18 years old.

UNITED STATES ECONOMIC AND MILITARY ASSISTANCE TO THAILAND, 1958–1967 (MILLIONS OF US DOLLARS)
* * * * * * *

Fiscal year	1958	1959	1960	1961	1962	1963	1964	1965	1966	1967
Economic	25.9	58.9	25.9	24.3	47.6	21.9	15.1	41.4	60.4	37.0
Military	19.7	18.0	24.7	49.0	88.0	71.8	35.2	30.8	42.3	59.0

Source: *Thailand: A Short History* by David Wyatt

METER, PLEASE
* * * * * * *

It is against the law for taxi drivers in Thailand to:

* refuse a passenger
* threaten a passenger
* put his hand, arm or any other part of his body out of the window when driving
* drive with one hand unless necessary
* honk the horn to speed other cars up
* carry more passengers than allowed by their licence (two children below the age of 10 may be counted as one adult)
* demand a fare higher than what the meter registers
* smoke or turn on music that annoys passengers
* drive onto private property without permission
* take an unnecessary detour
* drop off or abandon passengers in the middle of a journey

HOW TO PRAY IN A BUDDHIST TEMPLE
• • • • • •

- You will need candles, incense and flowers, which can be bought at the temple.
- Remove your shoes before entering the prayer area or chapel.
- Light candles and place them on the candleholders (two candles is standard, but it's also okay to light one).
- Light three incense sticks.
- Pray with the incense sticks and flowers (one can pray for anything and for any length of time).
- Place the incense sticks into the bowl in front of the Buddha image.
- Pay respect to the Buddha by prostrating yourself three times. You do this by kneeling with your hands pressed together in a *wai* position. Then leaning forward, you place your palms and forehead against the ground. Finally, return to a kneeling *wai* position. Your feet should never point toward the Buddha image.
- It is optional to fix gold leaf onto the Buddha statue. It is also optional to put oil into the lamps in the prayer area.

THE BUSINESS OF FORTUNE-TELLING
• • • • • •

Thais can be very superstitious; many believe that some people can predict the future, and that there is a good and bad day to perform a particular action. Some even change their first or last names to improve their fortunes. These superstitious beliefs have supported an industry of professional astrologers and fortune-tellers in Thailand for many years, an industry worth 4 billion baht (US$130 million) per year.

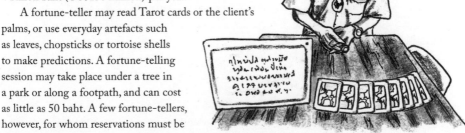

A fortune-teller may read Tarot cards or the client's palms, or use everyday artefacts such as leaves, chopsticks or tortoise shells to make predictions. A fortune-telling session may take place under a tree in a park or along a footpath, and can cost as little as 50 baht. A few fortune-tellers, however, for whom reservations must be made years in advance, charge millions of baht for a consultation.

Court astrologers are officially employed as civil servants under the Bureau of the Royal Household. There are presently 13 court astrologers who read the horoscope of the king and the royal family, and fix auspicious dates for sacred ceremonies and rituals.

RAMON MAGSAYSAY AWARD WINNERS
• • • • • • •

Established in 1957 by the Rockefeller Brothers Fund, the Ramon Magsaysay Awards, named after the former Philippine president, are given annually to Asians who demonstrate excellence in one of six categories: government service; public service; community leadership; journalism/literature/creative communication arts; peace and international understanding; and emerging leadership (first awarded in 2001). Twenty-one Thai individuals and two Thai organisations have received the prestigious honour.

Award recipient	Year	Award category
Nilawan Pinthong	1961	Public Service
Puey Ungphakorn	1965	Government Service
Phon Saengsingkeo	1966	Government Service
Sithiporn Kridakara	1967	Public Service
Prayoon Chanyavongs	1971	Journalism/Literature/Creative Communication Arts
Krasae Chanawongse	1973	Community Leadership
Phra Chamroon Parnchand	1975	Public Service
Prateep Ungsongtham-Hata	1978	Public Service
Prawase Wasi	1981	Government Service
Fua Hariphitak	1983	Public Service
Thongbai Thongpao	1984	Public Service
Aree Valyasevi	1987	Community Leadership
The Royal Project	1988	Peace and International Understanding
Asian Institute of Technology	1989	Peace and International Understanding
Princess Maha Chakri Sirindhorn	1991	Public Service
Chamlong Srimuang	1992	Government Service
Meechai Viravaidya	1994	Public Service
Anand Panyarachun	1997	Government Service
Sophon Suphapong	1998	Public Service
Prayong Ronnarong	2004	Community Leadership
Jon Ungphakorn	2005	Government Service
Therdchai Jivacate	2008	Public Service
Krisana Kraisintu	2009	Public Service

THE CHILLI: A GIFT FROM GOD
· · · · · ·

Introduced to Thailand in the 16th century by Portuguese missionaries, chillies, or *prik* as they are called in Thai, are used to add flavour and spice to Thai cuisine. One of the most popular kinds of Thai chilli, *prik khi nu* (literally "mouse dropping chilli") is among the spiciest, despite its relatively small size. *Prik khi nu*, besides packing a fiery kick, rewards eaters with high levels of vitamin C. Thai chillies are among the hottest in the world, second only to Latin America's scorching habanero peppers. Thais love to eat chillies for the taste, but they also consume them as a remedy for nasal congestion, blood clots and toothache as well as to reduce cholesterol.

LIVING ON STILTS
· · · · · ·

Before Western architecture became commonplace, Thais lived in traditional houses, which were built high above the ground on stilts. The empty space below the house could be used for several purpose—rearing the household's livestock, as a cleaning and washing area, or even as a playground for the children. Typical Thai houses usually have an outdoor space that functions like a veranda, where family members may gather and guests are received. A range of materials are used to construct different designs depending on the location of the house and the affluence of its owner. A basic Thai house is typically built with bamboo and dried nipa palm leaves, while wood is usually used for more complex structures.

GHOST BUILDINGS REVISITED
· · · · · · ·

W hen the economic crisis of 1997 hit Thailand, bankruptcies stopped the construction of some buildings mid-job. A 2001 survey revealed there were a total of 508 of these so-called "ghost buildings", prompting the Thai government to urge the financial institutions holding them to auction the buildings to private investors. As of 2012, 278 "ghost buildings" had been renovated and completed, and a further 25 are in the midst of being finished. Most of the remaining 205 buildings are expected to be completed by 2014.

Source: Real Estate Information Centre, Government Housing Bank

FOLK WISDOM IN THE KITCHEN
· · · · · · ·

Rule of etiquette	Justification	Consequence
A woman shouldn't sing while cooking.	Singing shows a lack of focus on cooking and also causes annoyance.	You will marry an old man.
Don't hit the rice pot when serving rice.	Old rice pots were made of clay and broke easily.	You will be born harelipped in the next life.
Don't let the fork and spoon hit each other and make noise when eating.	Making unnecessary noise is considered bad table manners.	Someone will bring bad news.
Don't eat while lying down.	Eating while lying down can make you choke.	You will be born as a snake in the next life.
Do not flip over the fish in the dish.	Flipping the fish in the dish is considered bad table manners.	Your boat will sink.

THE POWER OF A PHALLUS
· · · · · · ·

A mong the many types of talismans donned by Thais, none is quite as intriguing as the phallic one called *palad khik*. Worn off-centre at the waist by males, it is believed to protect against evil spirits and bring good fortune. Some Thais also put *palad khik* in front of their houses to deter the ghosts of widows from hunting them down and making them their husbands in the netherworld. Some shop owners will display the talisman near the cashier to promote prosperity. *Palad khik* may be carved from wood, animal horns or bones, or ivory. Some feature religious inscriptions.

OCCUPATIONS PROHIBITED TO FOREIGNERS
· · · · · · ·

U nder the Working of Aliens Act B.E. 2521 (1978), foreigners are prohibited from working in the following industries:

- Accounting/auditing, with the exception of part-time jobs
- Agriculture, forestry, fishery, and livestock ranching, with the exception of jobs requiring specialisation
- Architecture
- Auctioneering
- Brokering, with the exception of international trade jobs
- Clerical and secretarial work
- Construction
- Costume design
- Engineering, with the exception of jobs requiring specific expertise
- Gemstone cutting
- Goldsmithing, silversmithing, coppersmithing
- Hairdressing
- Labour, with the exception of jobs on fishing ships and foreigners from specific countries
- Law
- Manufacture of: cigarettes; Thai dolls; duvets and mattresses; hats; earthen-, lacquer-, niello-, stone- and polished metal- ware; alms bowls; handmade silk products; knives; shoes; Thai musical instruments; and umbrellas.
- Sales, especially jobs at shop counters and street stalls
- Tour guides
- Typesetting (by hand)
- Vehicle operation, with the exception of pilots
- Weaving, woodcraft, and papermaking by hand

EXTREME WEATHER
· · · · · · ·

H ighest recorded temperature: 44.5 degrees Celsius (112 Fahrenheit), Muang district, Uttaradit province, 27 April 1960.

Lowest recorded temperature: -1.4 degrees Celsius (29.5 Fahrenheit), Sakon Nakhon Agrometeorological Station, Sakon Nakhon province, 2 January 1974.

Source: Thai Meteorological Department

A SELECTION OF GRUESOME MURDERS
· · · · · · ·

Year	Description of crime	Outcome
1917	Boonpeng, a former monk at Wat Sutat, was charged with the murder of three people, each of whom was killed and placed inside a metal trunk, which was then sunk in a river.	Boonpeng was sentenced to death; he was the last Thai inmate to be decapitated.
1958	See Ooi Sae Eung, a Chinese immigrant, murdered an 8-year-old boy by cutting open his body and extracting his heart and liver allegedly with the intention of eating them. See Ooi also admitted to five similar crimes.	See Ooi was sentenced to death and was executed by gunshot.
1959	Railway Hospital doctor, Athip Suyansethakarn, murdered his wife, Nuanchawee Petchrung after incapacitating her with chloroform. His accomplice, Mongkol Rueruangrat, also stabbed and raped her.	Dr Athip was initially sentenced to death. After being imprisoned for 12 years, he received a royal pardon.
1975	The "Bikini Killer" Charles Sobhraj, along with two accomplices, killed five victims in Thailand by beating them to death or burning them alive. It is believed that he killed at least 12 Western tourists travelling on the so-called hippie trail.	He was arrested in India in 1976 and remained in an Indian prison until 1997. After his release, he went to Nepal and was arrested and sentenced to life in prison in 2004 for crimes he committed in Nepal.
1986	Sherry Ann Duncan, a beautiful 16-year-old Thai-American teenager, was strangled to death. Twenty-seven days later, the police arrested five suspects. One of them, her boyfriend Vinai Chaipanich, was released, while the other four were sentenced to death. In 1993, an appeal found them all to be innocent. However, one suspect had already died in prison. Two others died a few years after their release.	A reinvestigation in 1995 found that a girlfriend of Vinai had allegedly hired two men to kill Sherry Ann. She was convicted but then later released on appeal, while the two men she allegedly hired were sentenced to death.
1991	Klaew Thanikul, the Amateur Boxing Association's president and an alleged mafia boss, was murdered along with his bodyguard by an ambush of more than three gunmen, who attacked his car with rifles and hand grenades.	The perpetrators remain unknown. The killing came during a government crackdown on powerful mafia figures.
1998	Serm Sakornrat, a medical student, shot his girlfriend Janejira Ploi-angunsri, dismembered her dead body and flushed it down the toilet.	Serm was sentenced to life imprisonment. He was eventually pardoned and released on 18 December 2011.
2001	Dr Wisut Boonkasemsanti, a Chulalongkorn Hospital doctor, killed his wife, Dr Pasaporn, dismembered her dead body and flushed it down two different toilets.	The prosecuting attorney initially thought there was insufficient evidence and didn't file a case in court. Later Dr Pasaporn's father filed it and Dr Wisut was convicted.
2004	A 12-year-old girl's throat was cut by her mother and aunt as part of what the women believed was a ritual honouring the Hindu god Indra.	The two women were sent for psychiatric treatment at Galaya Rajanagarindra Institute.

THE ART OF BANANA LEAVES
· · · · · · ·

Banana leaves are commonly fashioned into containers. Craftwork using banana leaves originated in the Thai royal court. There are several types of containers that can be made from banana leaves:

- Food wrap. Common in the past before plastic was introduced, banana leaves have regained their popularity as food wraps for the environmentally conscious.
- Floral *krathong*. Used for religious and ceremonial purposes. Flowers, incense sticks and candles are stacked on top of the *krathong*.
- Floating *krathong*. Similar to the floral *krathong*, this is used during the *Loy Krathong* festival. Flowers, incense sticks and candles are floated down the river on the *krathong* to thank the river goddess Ganga.
- *Bai-sri*. Used to carry food or flowers and sometimes a mixture of both during ceremonies.

Food wrap   Floral *krathong*   Floating *krathong*   *Bai-sri*

ROYAL THAI ARMED FORCES OVERSEAS ENGAGEMENTS
· · · · · · ·

1917 – A Siamese Expeditionary Force joined Allied forces in Europe during World War I.

1950 – Royal Thai Armed Forces joined United Nations troops in the Korean peninsular.

1966 – Royal Thai Armed Forces assisted South Vietnam's government in the fight against communist North Vietnam.

1999 – Thai troops joined the International Force for East Timor (INTERFET) after widespread violence broke out in East Timor.

2003 – The Thai army joined the United States' building and medical assistance forces in Iraq after the Iraq War.

2010 – Royal Thai Armed Forces joined peacekeeping missions in the African Union/United Nations Hybrid Operation in Sudan.

THE WORLD'S MOST PROLIFIC ACTOR
· · · · · · ·

Thai heartthrob Sombat Methanee has appeared in more films than any other actor, a whopping 617 in total, according to *Guinness World Records*. Sombat started his acting career in a soap opera on Channel 7 in 1960. His first movie was *Rung Petch* in 1961. In the 1960s and 1970s, when there were few actors, a high demand for movies, and actors worked around the clock, he would feature (often in the lead role) in between 20 and 40 films per year. Sombat continued to appear in soap operas and films through the 2000s.

HOW TO GATHER BIRD SPIT
· · · · · · ·

Considered a delicacy in China and also popular among members of the Chinese diaspora, bird's nest soup contains the nests of swiftlets, which the birds construct with their saliva. Found mostly high on the walls of caves (but also in abandoned buildings), the nests are often extremely difficult to gather.

How the nest gatherers collect them:
1. Spray water onto the nests once they are abandoned by the swiftlets.
2. Use a trowel to gouge the nest out without damaging it.

How they process them:
1. Soak the nest in water for two hours.
2. Use tweezers to pick the feathers out.
3. Arrange the fibres onto a mould and fan until dry.

Interesting facts:
- The standard weight of a nest sold on the international market is six grammes.
- The nests can be sold at a price between 50,000 to 150,000 baht per kilogramme.
- In order to collect the nest from natural sources, the collector has to receive official permission from a governmental committee at the provincial level. Nests cannot be collected more than three times a year, and there are other restrictions to protect the birds, their eggs and nests.
- Nowadays, there are swiftlet farms where the birds are bred, often in abandoned buildings, for their nests; it has become a popular industry in Thailand.
- In Bangkok, a bowl of bird's nest soup costs on average around 600 baht (US$20).

Source: Swiftlet Research Center Co, Ltd

HAVE A HEART, MANY HEARTS
· · · · · ·

There are many adjectives and verbs in Thai that start or end with the word *jai* (heart). In order to express emotion and describe people, the word *jai* has been incorporated into many different phrases and idioms.

Phrase	Combination of …	Meaning
jai dee	heart + good	kind, generous
jai rai	heart + bad	mean, cruel
jai dum	heart + black	mean, cruel
jai ngai	heart + easy	gullible
jai ron	heart + hot	hot-tempered
jai yen	heart + cool	calm, serene
jai on	heart + soft	sensitive
jai khaeng	heart + hard	adamant
jai noi	heart + little	easily offended
jai yai	heart + big	ostentatious
plaek jai	strange + heart	to be surprised
dee jai	good + heart	happy
sia jai	bad + heart	sad
kreng jai	afraid + heart	to be considerate
hen jai	see + heart	to be sympathetic
jing jai	true + heart	sincere
khao jai	enter + heart	to understand
tuk jai	correct + heart	to like
tok jai	fall + heart	to be shocked

READING RATES
· · · · · ·

The 2000 census put the Thai literacy rate at 92.6%. On average, a Thai:
- reads 5 books per year
- buys 2 books per year
- reads for 39 minutes per day

Source: Thai Library Association

THE GIANT CROCODILE HUNT
· · · · · · ·

In 1964, a giant man-eating crocodile was the subject of sensational headlines in local tabloids. Known as *Ai Dang*, the massive crocodile devoured a man in Klong Bangmut in Chumphon province. The name *Ai Dang* (which means "spotted") came from its mottled appearance: the black croc had a white stripe on its neck.

Hunters set out to kill the crocodile several times without success. Some managed to shoot *Ai Dang*, but the reptile survived. Finally, three C3 clay bombs were dropped into the water, and when *Ai Dang* emerged in reaction to the explosions, one of the hunters shot the crocodile through its neck with a harpoon. The crocodile's remains were sold for 23,000 baht, preserved and displayed at freak shows. From head to tail, the crocodile measured 4.25 metres, with a waist of 1.75 metres. When wide open, its mouth was 20 inches wide. Two human skulls and numerous bones were found inside the crocodile's stomach.

The magnificent story of the hunt for *Ai Dang* has been adapted into two films, released in 1988 and in 2005.

PIBUL'S NATIONALISM
· · · · · · ·

During Field Marshal Pibul Songgram's first term as prime minister, he made 12 public orders in the name of promoting nationalism and national identity. For example, Pibul changed the country's name from Siam to Thailand (which means "Land of the Free") and instructed the public to adopt certain styles of dress. One particularly notable declaration, issued on 8 September 1941, concerned people's daily activities. It stated the following:

- Thai citizens should divide their time into three parts: one part for work, the other two for personal activities and rest.
- Thai citizens should eat no more than four meals a day, always at the same time, and sleep between six and eight hours per night.
- Thai citizens should work diligently and not avoid their responsibilities. Lunch breaks should not be longer than one hour. Free time outside of work should be spent on outdoor exercise (at least one hour per day). Otherwise, free time should be spent on useful activities like planting vegetables, raising livestock and growing trees. Showers should be taken before each meal.
- Evenings should be spent on unfinished work or in conversation with family members and friends, or gaining new knowledge from radio programmes, books or other forms of entertainment.
- Holidays should be spent for the benefit of one's physical and mental health through activities like religious practice, study, travel, sports and relaxation.

HOW A TIN DREDGE WORKED
· · · · · · ·

Tin was one of the pillars of the old economy before the industry collapsed. The most effective and capital intensive method of mining alluvial tin, tin dredges were used in Phuket and other areas in the south that had tin deposits. Tin dredges are no longer used in Thailand.

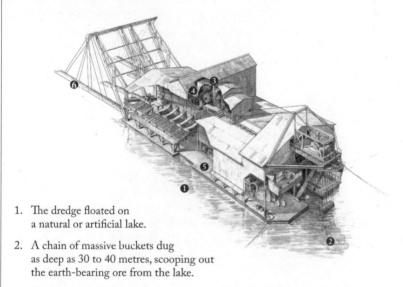

1. The dredge floated on a natural or artificial lake.

2. A chain of massive buckets dug as deep as 30 to 40 metres, scooping out the earth-bearing ore from the lake.

3. The earth-bearing ore was carried to a high point in the body of the dredge.

4. The excavated material was broken up by jets of water as it fell onto revolving or oscillating screens. Large stones and rubble were retained by these screens while material bearing tin ore passed through the holes in the screen and was collected in a tank below the screens. The tin ore was then separated, using water pumps, from foreign matter and cleaned.

5. The purified tin ore was collected in drums to be transported from the dredge to the treatment plant.

6. Mud, sand, clay and gravel were discharged with the main flow of water and were dumped in the tailings area at the rear of the dredge.

BAD LUCK BUFFALO
· · · · · · ·

Buffalo can be seen almost everywhere in Thailand, and rural Thais have been dependent on this beast of burden for generations. Owing to this fact, there are quite a few superstitions about what makes a good or bad buffalo. Here are the meanings of some of the more inauspicious characteristics.

Characteristic	Implication
White spots on four parts of the body (forehead, hoof, tail, and mouth)	It should not be killed or sold by its owner, and is better to use on land that is haunted by evil spirits.
Black tongue (top or bottom or both) or snores	It will bring misfortune to the owner.
Disfigured testicles, black ear lobes	Stubborn, cannot be trusted and can harm the owner.
Has a hole in the front tooth	It will likely be stolen.
Grinds teeth while sleeping	It will bring bad luck and will get sick.
White tail	Selling it will lead to bad luck.

THE LIFE OF A PRISONER
· · · · · · ·

There are a total of 185 prisons and correctional institutions across Thailand. Of these, one is a hospital, seven have drug rehabilitation facilities, and 23 are temporary confinement centres. There are also four open correctional institutions in which convicts who have nearly completed their sentence are allowed to move more freely.

According to the Department of Corrections, prisoners in Thailand have the right to three nutritious meals daily, free medical treatment as necessary, religious freedom, and contact with the outside world through visits from their relatives and lawyers, written letters, email (in certain prisons), television, radio, and newspapers. A few prisons allow visits every working day, but most have specified visiting days and times.

Prisoners are also entitled to proper accommodation. Compared to the international standard for sleeping space per prisoner (7.5 square metres), the official standard in Thailand is 2.5 square metres, which is still considered acceptable in a room with proper ventilation. However, overpopulation in prisons means that on average, each prisoner has only 0.85 square metres to sleep in, a space that is three times smaller than the official national requirement.

Source: Department of Corrections

A "SHORT-TIME" HISTORY OF PROSTITUTION
· · · · · · ·

Thailand has an international reputation as a place of rampant prostitution, an image that rankles many Thais who say that the world's oldest profession is practised in every country in the world. Several misconceptions about the prostitution industry persist, including the idea that American GIs were responsible for its introduction to Thailand during the Vietnam War era of the 1960s and 1970s. As far back as the reign of King Chulalongkorn, prostitution was already creating public health concerns. The king's Diseases Prevention Act B.E. 2451 (1908) was formed, in part, to regulate and register every brothel and prostitute. The Act also ordered every brothel to hang a lantern outside in order to indicate its business. By the 1920s, go-go bars had developed out of the Chinatown cabarets.

The Prohibition of Prostitution Act B.E. 2503 (1960) superseded the 1908 Act and made prostitution illegal. The fine for those involved with prostitution was 1,000 baht, three months imprisonment or both. This Act was later revised as the Prevention and Suppression of Prostitution Act B.E. 2539 (1996), which states that a person involved in prostitution will be fined 1,000 baht, receive one month imprisonment or both.

Today, prostitution is often transacted at entertainment or massage businesses, including massage parlours, call girl/hostess services, *ramwong* bars, karaoke bars and other "grey area" establishments. Statistics from the police show that in 2011 19,925 people were arrested for violating the Prevention and Suppression of Prostitution Act B.E. 2539. The incident rate was highest in December and January. Estimates about the number of prostitutes vary wildly as they are not registered, and few would define their work as such. A United Nations Population Fund report from 2006 estimated there were 55,355 female and 4,460 male prostitutes in Thailand.

WHY ARE THOSE TISSUES PINK?
· · · · · · ·

Why are the ubiquitous tiny napkins found on tabletops at restaurants throughout the country invariably pink? The colour indicates that the napkins are made from recycled paper, and the colour disguises this fact. These napkins are slightly cheaper than new, bleached white napkins, meaning precious savings for your food cart vendor or shophouse restaurant for this customer giveaway. The pink comes from food colouring extracts. But why not a less flashy colour? Originally, they did come in several colours, including yellow and blue, but the pink colour prevailed due it its popularity at Chinese banquets at which red and pink are auspicious colours.

Sources: *Very Thai: Everyday Popular Culture* by Philip Cornwel-Smith and a former executive at a tissue company

BANGKOK TRAM TRIVIA
· · · · · · ·

For 80 years, trams plied Bangkok's main streets and one service went to Paknam. The trams were called either *rot tram* (tram cars) or *rot ai* (*ai* means vapour; this is a reference to the sweat and heat as people were packed tightly into the trams). Here are some facts about the Bangkok tram system:

Track lengths
Total distance (Lines 1 through 7)	42 km
Paknam Railway	21 km
Total distance of electric mass transit line	63 km

Size
A tram car was 2 x 8 metres and driven by a 40-60 HP motor. Locally made trams were constructed from teak while imported versions were made from aluminium.

Timeline
- 22 September 1888 – Alfred John Loftus (aka Phraya Nithetcholthee) opens a horse-drawn tramway line from City Pillar to Thanon Tok
- 11 April 1893 – The Paknam Railway opens for service
- May 1894 – Electrified tramway service with Belgian and German rolling stock and electric power from Siam Electricity Co Ltd, a Danish public utility company, was introduced. The street cars were painted yellow.
- September 1901 – Samsen–Hua Lamphong line opens, powered by Bangkok Electric Light Syndicate Co Ltd (later Samsen Power Plant)
- 1 October 1905 – Bang Lamphoo–Hua Lamphong line opens for service with King Chulalongkorn presiding over the opening ceremony. This line was controlled by Siamese Tramways Co Ltd founded by Prince Narathip Pongpraphan.
- 1 January 1950 – Nationalised to Bangkok Municipal and the Department of Civil Works; the Ministry of Interior runs the services.
- 19 December 1961 – Cabinet resolution states that all Bangkok tramways must close for the larger good of commuter traffic under a gradual phase-out plan. Over the next seven years, lines are closed one by one.
- 1 October 1968 - Bangkok tramway system ceases operations
- After the service was terminated, the Metropolitan Electric Authority transferred the tram workers and sold the steel rails to junkyards for 50 satang (half a baht) per kilogramme

Source: www.2bangkok.com

GHOSTBUSTING
· · · · · ·

Ask a Thai if they believe in ghosts (*phi*) and the majority will say yes. Some might even regale you with a story from their own lives. Ghost stories have long formed a part of the oral culture, and have typically acted as morality tales. Here are some examples of the more than 40 typical Thai ghosts.

Phi tai tang klom

Kra sue

Name	Form it assumes
kra sue	A floating female head with dangling entrails. She usually comes out at night to eat raw fowl and waste.
kra hang	An ordinary man with a small tail who can fly at night. He is associated with black magic.
nang tani	A beautiful female ghost that dwells in *tani* banana trees. It is believed that *nang tani* likes to seduce men; then, once a man moves on to another girl, the ghost kills him.
nang takian	This is a beautiful female ghost that lives in *takian* trees (which are often used for making boats and houses). When a boat or house is made from the *takian* tree, *nang takian* will become *mae ya nang* (the guardian spirit) of the vessel.
pob	If someone is practising black magic and it goes wrong, she or he might transform into a *pob*. A *pob* has an insatiable hunger for raw meat and doesn't die until it transfers its possessed nature to another family member.
petra	*Petra* is as tall as a palm tree, skinny with a big belly, and has long hair. His skin is dark and his mouth is as small as a needle's eye. When you meet *petra*, he usually asks for merit.
phi tai tang klom	This is the ghost of a woman who was pregnant or giving birth at the time of her death.
phi tai hong	This is the ghost of a person who has died suddenly. He usually dwells at the spot where he died and waits for someone to die there so that he can be reborn.
phi kong koi	A one-legged ghost with a tube-shaped mouth who lives in the forest. He usually hops around on one leg and sucks people's blood from their toes.

Source: *Very Thai: Everyday Popular Culture* by Philip Cornwel-Smith

BASKET CASES
· · · · · · ·

Used to trap fish, hold rice or store your lunch, a basket has many functions in Thailand. Given that they are cheap to construct and can be made from widely available natural materials (bamboo, reeds, rattan or grass), this is not surprising. But not every basket looks alike. Here are some common types:

Type	Where it's common	Purpose	Design
Rice basket or *krabung*	Every region in Thailand	To store, carry and measure rice	There are loops through which a pole can be placed so that two *krabung* can be carried at once
Glutinous rice basket or *kratip*	Northern and northeastern parts of Thailand	Used as a lunch box by farmers	The bottom is made from wood, which raises the basket off the ground and thus prevents contact with dirt. An attached cord acts as a handle, making it easy to carry.
Water basket or *mah* (or *timah*)	Southern part of Thailand	To store water from natural sources or wells	A wooden handle makes it easy to carry
Duck-shaped basket or *takhong pet*	Every region in Thailand	To trap fish	An attached string, which acts as a handle, makes it easy to transport

NOT THE CHEAPEST CAB IN THE WORLD
· · · · · · ·

A taxi ride in Bangkok is among the cheapest in the world. A survey of 72 big cities determined the cost of a three-kilometre ride during light and heavy traffic. The lower figure reflects the price without traffic and higher figure with heavy traffic. Bangkok was the 14th cheapest ride in the world. The three most expensive? Zurich, Oslo and Monaco in that order. The cheapest were as follows (in US dollars):

$0.90 – $1.58	Delhi, India
$0.97 – $1.29	Mumbai, India
$1.01 – $1.68	Cairo, Egypt
$1.15 – $1.73	La Paz, Bolivia
$1.16 – $1.85	Manila, Philippines
$1.25 – $3.00	Panama City, Panama
$1.27 – $1.73	Kuta, Bali, Indonesia
$1.28 – $1.91	Fez, Morocco
$1.29 – $2.14	Mexico City, Mexico
$1.32 – $1.98	Kuala Lumpur, Malaysia
$1.43 – $1.91	Ho Chi Minh City, Vietnam
$1.53 – $3.06	Beijing, China
$1.53 – $1.91	Hanoi, Vietnam
$1.66 – $2.32	**Bangkok, Thailand**
$1.69 – $3.38	Kathmandu, Nepal

Source: www.priceoftravel.com; prices determined in April 2011.

BEFORE IT WAS A RED-LIGHT DISTRICT ...
· · · · · · ·

Patpong – Formerly a banana plantation, this plot was purchased by the Patpongpanich family in 1946 for 60,000 baht (US$2,400 at the time). The family made a cut-through street (now called Patpong 1) over its land to link the two parallel thoroughfares of Silom and Surawong roads. It once contained the offices of major international companies such as Shell, Air France, Qantas and IBM, but it was also developed as a nightlife zone. By the late 1960s, American GIs had made it a popular destination during their R&R visits.

Nana Plaza – Initially started as a shop and restaurant complex in the late 1970s. The leases were gradually taken over by go-go bars and short-time hotels in the 1980s. By the 1990s, it had become an internationally famous destination.

Soi Cowboy – This small lane was named for T.G. Edwards, a former American air force officer who opened the first bar there in 1977 and was fond of wearing cowboy hats.

ALL THE THAI PRIME MINISTERS
· · · · · · ·

I n 1932, Thailand's absolute monarchy was replaced by a constitutional monarchy after a military coup. Since then the country's parliamentary system has been marked by chronic political instability, save for a few stretches when unelected prime ministers ran the country. Indeed, it was not until the 2000s, during the office of Thaksin Shinawatra, that any elected Thai prime minister lasted his full term.

Prime minister	Dates	How term ended
Phraya Manopakornnitiitthada	1932–1933	Removed through a coup
General Phraya Phahol Pholphayuhasena	1933–1938	Resigned
Field Marshal Pibul Songgram	1938–1944 1948–1957	Resigned Removed through a coup
Major Khuang Aphaiwong	1944–1945 January–March 1946 November 1947–April 1948	Resigned Resigned Removed through a coup
Tawee Bunyaket	1945 (17 days)	Resigned
Mom Rajawongse Seni Pramoj	September 1945–January 1946 February–March 1975 April–September 1976 September–October 1976	Resigned Resigned Resigned Removed through a coup
Pridi Bamonyong	March–August 1946	Resigned
Rear Admiral Thawal Thamrongnawasawat	August 1946–November 1947	Removed through a coup
Pote Sarasin	September–December 1957	Resigned
Field Marshal Thanom Kittikachorn	January–October 1958 December 1963–October 1973	Resigned Resigned and went into exile

TRAGEDY ON THE ROADS
· · · · · · ·

T here were 68,582 road accidents in Thailand in 2011, causing 9,185 deaths and injuring 16,564 people. Bangkok was the site of 40,250 of these accidents, which caused 785 deaths and injured 3,752.

Source: Royal Thai Police

Field Marshal Sarit Thanarat	1959–1963	Deceased
Sanya Dharmasakti	1973–1975	Resigned
Mom Rajawongse Kukrit Pramoj	March 1975–January 1976	Dissolution of Parliament
Thanin Kraivixien	October 1976–March 1977	Removed through a coup
General Kriangsak Chomanand	1977–1980	Resigned
General Prem Tinsulanonda	1980–1988	Dissolution of Parliament
General Chatichai Choonhavan	1988–1991	Removed through a coup
Anand Panyarachun	March 1991–March 1992 June 1992–September 1992	Resigned Resigned
General Suchinda Kraprayoon	April 1992–May 1992	Resigned
Chuan Leekpai	1992–1995 1997–2000	Dissolution of Parliament Dissolution of Parliament
Banharn Silpa-Archa	July 1995–September 1996	Dissolution of Parliament
General Chaovalit Yongchaiyuth	November 1996–November 1997	Resigned
Thaksin Shinawatra	2001–2006	Removed through a coup
General Surayud Chulanont	2006–2008	Resigned
Samak Sundaravej	January 2008–September 2008	Decision by the Constitutional Court ended term.
Somchai Wongsawat	September–December 2008	Dissolution of People's Power Party by the Constitutional Court's ended term.
Abhisit Vejjajiva	2008–2011	Dissolution of Parliament
Yingluck Shinawatra	2011–	Current

COST OF A SEX CHANGE OPERATION
· · · · · · ·

For a man to become a woman, the typical sex change operation costs 240,000 baht (US$7,770). For a woman to become a man, it's more than twice as expensive, 580,000 baht (US$18,780). Yanhee Hospital performs on average 300 sex change operations per year.

Source: Yanhee Hospital

ON INTERPOL'S WANTED LIST
· · · · · · ·

As of September 2012, there were 16 Thai nationals listed on Interpol's wanted list. Three of them were women. Their crimes cover the following categories: counterfeiting, sex crimes, drug-related crimes, human trafficking and illegal immigration, kidnapping, organised/transnational crime, life and health crimes (e.g. murder) and terrorism. About half are listed as wanted by either the US or Australian police.

Source: Interpol

ROYAL PLOUGHING CEREMONY
· · · · · · ·

Each May, on a day that court astrologers have declared auspicious, two significant events are held to bless the nation's crop production. The first, a Buddhist ceremony for blessing seeds, is conducted at the Temple of the Emerald Buddha and involves a prediction for the year's crop yields. Meanwhile, a Brahmin ceremony occurs both in Sanam Luang and at a paddy field in Chitralada Villa. In Sanam Luang, the Ploughing Lord, or *Phraya Raek Na*, wears an ancient Brahmin uniform and serves as master of ceremonies, leading royal oxen and celestial maidens in a symbolic ploughing. The role of Ploughing Lord is generally assumed by the Permanent Secretary of the Ministry of Agriculture and Cooperatives. At the ceremony two predictions are made. The Ploughing Lord chooses between three lengths of loincloth to predict the season's rainfall:

- If he chooses a loincloth with a length of four palm spans there will be too much rainfall.
- If he chooses a loincloth with a length of five palm spans there will be an ideal amount of rainfall.
- If he chooses a loincloth with a length of six palm spans there will be too little rainfall.

In addition, food is placed in front of the royal oxen. Their selections result in another prediction for the year.

- If they choose the plate with unmilled rice or corn, it means that rice and fruit cultivation will be bountiful.
- If they choose green beans or sesame, it means that rice and fruit cultivation will be average.
- If they choose water or grass, it means there will be an ideal amount of water for cultivating crops.
- If they choose rice wine, it means there will be healthy trade and a strong economy throughout the year.

MISS UNIVERSE 1965 VERSUS MISS UNIVERSE 1988

· · · · · · ·

	Apasara Hongsakul (1965)	Porntip Narkhirunkanok (1988)
Nickname	Pook	Pui
Age when she won	18	19
Height	163 cm	172 cm
Weight	52 kg	51 kg
Hometown	Bangkok	Chachoengsao
Host city	Miami Beach, Florida	Taipei, Taiwan
Quote	"I never dreamed of this. I pray to Buddha every night before I go to sleep. Last night I prayed, not to win, but that I might be one of the top five."	"I have a big responsibility to myself, to my family, to my country, and the universe."
First runner-up	Virpi Miettinen from Finland	Chang Yoonjung from Korea
Future family life	Married and divorced a relative of Queen Sirikit, second marriage to Thai billionaire ended in divorce, two sons from two marriages	Married an American billionaire, and has one son and one daughter
Future profession	Owner of Apasara's Beauty Slimming Spa	Housewife, with commercial endorsements and occasional charitable projects

RAMWONG
• • • • • • •

The reason that the dance is called *ramwong* is simple. *Ram* means dance and *wong* means circle. It is standard for the dancers to group together and dance in a circle. *Ramwong* is adapted from the original folk dance called *ramthone*. It featured Thai musical instruments such as cymbals (*ching*), Thai castanet (*krab*) and small drums (*thone*). In 1944, the government, through the Fine Arts Department, standardised the dance with a combination of Thai classical dancing postures and the use of Western musical instruments to transform it into *ramwong*.

SUKHOTHAI INSCRIPTION NO. 1
• • • • • • •

The famous engraving known as Sukhothai Inscription No. 1 was discovered in 1833 by the future King Mongkut when he was still a monk and then brought to Bangkok. Dated 1292 (from the reign of King Ramkamhaeng), it is the first record of the Thai alphabet and the earliest of several chronicles from the kingdom of Sukhothai that detail the lineage, deeds and achievements of its rulers. Several historians dispute the origins of the inscription, believing that it dates from a later time, or is a forgery. A passage from Sukhothai Inscription No. 1:

"In the time of King Ramkamhaeng this land of Sukhothai is thriving. There are fish in the water and rice in the fields. The lord of the realm does not levy toll on his subjects for travelling the roads; they lead their cattle to trade or ride their horses to sell; whoever wants to trade in elephants, does so; whoever wants to trade in horses, does so; whoever wants to trade in gold and silver, does so. When any commoner or man of rank dies, his estate—his elephants, wives, children, granaries, rice, retainers and groves of areca and betel—is left in its entirety to his son. When commoners or men of rank differ and disagree, [the king] examines the case to get at the truth and then settles it justly for them. He does not connive with thieves or favour concealers [of stolen goods]. When he sees someone's rice he does not covet it, when he sees someone's wealth he does not get angry ... He has hung a bell in the opening of the gate over there: if any commoner in the land has a grievance which sickens his belly and troubles his heart, and which he wants to make known to his ruler and lord, it is easy; he goes and strikes the bell which the king has hung there; King Ramkamhaeng, the ruler of the kingdom, hears the call; he goes and questions the man, examines the case, and decides it justly for him. So the people of this mueang of Sukhothai praise him."

TOP TEN THAI EXPORTS
• • • • • • •

1. Cars and car-related equipment and components .... 384.7 billion baht
2. Computers and computer-related equipment and components .... 354.7 billion baht
3. Petroleum products .... 232.1 billion baht
4. Jewels .... 210.5 billion baht
5. Rubber .... 167.5 billion baht
6. Plastic granules .... 154.3 billion baht
7. Chemical products .... 152.7 billion baht
8. Rubber products .... 152 billion baht
9. Circuit boards .... 116.5 billion baht
10. Machinery and machinery-related components .... 111.9 billion baht

Most famous for being one of the leading exporters of rice in the world, Thailand has moved away from agriculture and toward manufacturing in the last two decades. Today, the country relies especially on its car and computer production.

Source: Thailand Trading Report by Ministry of Commerce; covering period from January to July 2012.

BRIDGES OVER THE CHAO PHRAYA RIVER
• • • • • • •

The Chao Phraya is Thailand's most famous river. Passing through the heart of the capital and spilling into the Gulf of Thailand by Samut Prakan province, the 370-kilometre-long river is a major passageway for commercial boats such as rice barges, as well as commuter traffic. There are a total of 19 bridges built across the Chao Phraya in Bangkok and the vicinity. Here they are, in the order of year of construction:

- Rama IV Bridge (1926)
- Memorial Bridge (1933)
- Krungthon Bridge (1957)
- Khungthep Bridge (1959)
- Nonthaburi Bridge (1959)
- Phra Pinklao Bridge (1973)
- Taksin Bridge (1982)
- Pathumthani Bridge (1984)
- Phra Pokklao Bridge (1984)
- Phra Nungklao Bridge (1985)

- Rama VII Bridge (1992)
- Rama IX Bridge (1997)
- Rama III Bridge (2000)
- Rama IV Bridge (2002)
- Rama VIII Bridge (2002)
- Industrial Ring Road Bridge (2006)
- Kanchanapisek Bridge (2007)
- New Phra Nungklao Bridge (2008)
- Nakhon Nonthaburi Bridge (2011)

HOLLYWOOD GOES THAI
· · · · · · ·

English title	Thai title	Translation
The Terminator	*Kon lek 2029*	Iron man 2029
I Am Sam	*Su pab burut punya nim*	The retarded gentleman
Cast Away	*Kon lud lok*	Man who fell off the earth
No Country for Old Men	*La kon du nai muang duead*	Hunting fierce men in a fierce town
Resident Evil	*Pi chi wa*	Biology ghost
Kill Bill	*Nangfa samurai*	Samurai angel
Hollow Man	*Manut rai ngao*	Shadow-less man
Gone with the Wind	*Vimarn loy*	Floating paradise
Brokeback Mountain	*Hup kao ren rak*	Mountain of hidden love
Life is Beautiful	*Yim wai lok ni mai mi sin wang*	Smile and the world will have no despair

MOST COMMON CAUSES OF DEATH
· · · · · · ·

Top five common causes of death in Thailand (in 2009):

1. Cancers and tumours (all forms)
2. Accidents and poisoning (excluding suicide and homicide)
3. Heart disease
4. Hypertension and cerebrovascular disease
5. Pneumonia and other lung diseases

Source: Health Information Unit, Bureau of Health Policy and Strategy, Ministry of Public Health

BATTLING DRUG ADDICTION
· · · · · · ·

A study conducted in October 2011 revealed that there are approximately 1.3 million people in Thailand who are addicted to drugs, or nearly 2% of the population. This figure is six times higher than the international standard. The youngest person found abusing drugs was a 9-year-old amphetamine addict.

Source: *Thai Post* newspaper (28 December 2011)

THE ROCKET FESTIVAL
· · · · · · ·

The Rocket Festival (or *Bun Bang Fai* in Thai) is a festival held in the northeastern provinces of Thailand, and is an especially popular and large event in the province of Yasothon. The festival usually takes place during the second week of May at the beginning of the rainy season before farmers plant their crops. The participants shoot rockets into the sky to encourage rainfall. The practise originates from the legend of *Vassakan*, the rain god, who enjoyed being worshipped with fire. Therefore, farmers shoot rockets into the heavens where *Vassakan* resides. The festival involves traditional dancing, floats, beauty pageants, signing, continuous drinking and partying, and on the final day, the ignition of the rockets.

Created by teams of "technicians" over a period of weeks and then decorated, an average homemade rocket is around 9 metres in length and carries 20-25 kilogrammes of gunpowder. They can be as long as almost 20 metres, however, and packed with as much as 130 kilogrammes of gunpowder. In the past, the rocket was made from bamboo, but now people often use metal or PVC piping. When set off, they can fly hundreds of metres into the air and often completely out of sight. Even flight control towers in the vicinity are alerted so the affected air space is clear of traffic. The festival has seen its share of accidents over the years, including some fatalities caused by misfires.

SOME POLITICAL PARTY NAMES TRANSLATED
• • • • • • •

- *Taen Khun Paendin Isaan* .... Gratitude to Isaan
- *Tian Hang Thum* .... Candlelight of Wisdom
- *Pua Piang* .... Sufficiency
- *Ton Trakun Thai* .... Thai Ancestors
- *Ngern Duean Prachachon* .... Citizen's Income
- *Kru Thai Puea Prachachon* .... Thai Teachers for the People
- *Palang Kon Kila* .... Power of Sportsmen
- *Rak Prathet Thai* .... Love Thailand
- *Rao Puean Kun* .... We are Friends
- *Thai Than Thun* .... Thai Capital Awareness
- *Thai Sangsan* .... Creative Thailand
- *Thai Pen Suk* .... Happy Thai
- *Araya Thum* .... Civilisation
- *Rak Paendin* .... Love the Land
- *Sang Thai* .... Build Thailand
- *Yang Para Thai* .... Thai Rubber
- *Chewit Thi Di Kwa* .... Better Life
- *Puea Fa Din* .... For Heaven and Earth
- *Anakot Thai* .... Thai Future

THE HARMONY OF LIGHT BANTER
• • • • • • •

"To each other everyone is outwardly polite, even lighthearted, but they are rarely frank. Because the other person is superior or inferior, he must be treated circumspectly, particularly if he is a stranger for he may become the source of some advantage or disadvantage. Even those of long acquaintance may not be trusted implicitly, for they too may lead one to catastrophe. From this atmosphere arises the Thai proclivity to maximise the harmony and pleasantness of meeting others: it is well to avoid debates and best to keep the topic amusingly light. Because of unseen dangers, a leader ordinarily avoids giving benefits to strangers, and a potential member of a group must be introduced by a known person. Similarly, a liaison between superior and inferior once established needs continual validation, be it merely through the smile of a servant or the commendation of a master."

–From L.M. Hanks's pioneering anthropological essay "Merit and Power in the Thai Social Order", published in *American Anthropologist*, in 1962.

THE HIT PARADE
· · · · · · ·

"**B**ird" Thongchai McIntyre is the most successful Thai pop singer of all-time. He has seven albums that have sold more than one million copies each. They are:
- Boomerang (1990)
- *Prik khee nu* (1991)
- *Thor thong* (1994)
- Thongchai Service (1998)
- *Tu pleng samun prajum ban* (1999)
- Smile Club (2001)
- *Rab kaek* (2002)

"Bird" Thongchai McIntyre

In addition to these albums by Bird, the following bands or artists released albums that went on to sell more than a million copies:

- Grand Ex – Luktoong Disco (1) (1979), Grand X.O. (1981)
- Sornpetch Pinyo and Nongnuch Duangchewan – *Noom nakao sao nakluer* (1981)
- Sayan Sunya – *Kwamrak muen yakom* (1982)
- Carabao – Made in Thailand (1984), Welcome to Thailand (1987)
- Danuphon Kaewkarn – *Fan sithong* (1986)
- Pornsak Songsang – *Toey saochan kungkob* (1986)
- Pimpa Pornsiri – *Namta mia Saudi* (1987)
- Nuveau – *Pen yungngee tangtae kerd laey* (1988)
- Asanee-Wasan – *Fak thong* (1989), *Sapparot* (1990)
- Nick Niranam – *Yib sib* (1989)
- O-phas Thotsaporn – *Pleng warn super classic* (1990)
- Samthone – *Ab sanook sanan kub kwam mungmun kong chewit* (1990)
- Two – *Rak luan luan tae kuan na* (1991)
- Amphon Lampoon – *Wattu wai fai* (1992)
- Christina Aguilar – Ninja (1990), Red Beat (1994), Golden Eyes (1997)
- Mai Charoenpura – *Kwam lub sud khob fa* (1992), *Plaeng rit* (1998)
- Mos Patiphan – *Mr Mos mai rak mai dai laew* (1994)
- Amita Tata Young – *Sao noi mahatsachan* (1995)
- Beau Sunita – Beau (1996)
- Joey Boy – Fun Fun Fun (1997)
- James Ruangsak – Siren Love (1997)
- Pookie Prisna – Wonderful (1997)
- Parn Thanaporn – *Warn pha sak* (2001)
- D2B – D2B (2001), Type II (2003)
- I-Nam – *Rak kon mee jao khong* (2004)
- Ponglang sa-orn – *Ponglang sa-orn the Music* (2006)

Source: *Seesan* magazine

ICONIC THAILAND
. . . .

Distinctive objects and products that are a common part of everyday life for many Thais:

Noodle spoon

Inhaler

Bottle of fish sauce

Khan (metal bowl for water)

Can of Prickly Heat Powder

Bottle of soy sauce

Mortar and pestle

Metal *binto* (lunchbox)

DEFINITION OF ABSOLUTE ROYAL POWER
• • • • • • •

"The king rules absolutely at his own royal desire. There is nothing greater than this. The king has absolute power as 1) ruler over the realm and refuge for the people 2) the source of justice 3) the source of rank and status 4) commander of the armed forces who relieves the people's suffering by waging war or conducting friendly relations with other countries. The king can do no wrong. There is no power that can judge or punish him."–Definition by King Chulalongkorn (r. 1868–1910)

Source: Attachak Sattayanurak, *Change in the Thai Elite's Worldview from the Fourth Reign to 1932*, page 151, as quoted in *A History of Thailand* by Chris Baker and Pasuk Phongpaichit

KEY GENERAL DEMOGRAPHICS
• • • • • • •

Population	69,518,555 (2011)
0–14 years old	12,371,252 (2010)
60 years old and above	7,493,227 (2010)
Population density per square kilometre (Bangkok)	5,258.6 (2010)
Population density per square kilometre (whole kingdom)	127.5 (2010)
Births	765,047 (2009)
Deaths	393,916 (2009)
Marriages	285,944 (2010)
Divorces	108,482 (2010)

Sources: World Bank, National Statistical Office of Thailand

SELECTED WILDLIFE-RELATED CRIMES AND PUNISHMENTS
• • • • • • •

Killing a python – violators are fined up to 40,000 baht and/or receive four years imprisonment.

Breeding a leopard – violators are fined up to 30,000 baht and/or receive three years of imprisonment.

Unlawful possession of an elephant – violators are fined up to 40,000 baht and/or receive four years imprisonment.

Unlawful sale of long-tailed macaque monkeys – violators are fined up to 40,000 baht and/or receive four years imprisonment.

Source: Wildlife Preservation and Protection Act B.E. 2535 (1992)

ENDANGERED SPECIES
· · · · · · ·

The Wild Animal Preservation and Protection Act B.E. 2535 (1992) listed 15 species as endangered. These animals cannot be hunted, bred, imported, or exported without special permission from the government. The protected animals are as follows:

- white-eyed river martin
- Javan rhino
- Sumatran rhino
- kouprey
- Asiatic or wild water buffalo
- brow-antlered deer
- Schomburgk's deer
- serow
- grey Chinese goral
- black-breasted pitta
- east sarus crane
- marbled cat
- Malayan tapir
- fea's barking deer
- dugong

Fea's barking deer

Kouprey

TRADITIONAL WEIGHTS AND MEASUREMENTS
· · · · · · ·

The traditional system of weights is almost never used anymore, except in relation to gold (specifically *baht*). The lengths and area measures, however, are still commonly referred to.

Weights
1 *baht* = 15 grammes
1 *chang luang* = 600 grammes
1 *harb luang* = 60 kilogrammes

Areas
1 square *wa* = 4 square metres
1 *ngan* = 400 square metres
1 *rai* = 1,600 square metres

Lengths
1 *keub* = 25 centimetres
1 *sok* = 50 centimetres
1 *la* = 3 feet
1 *wa* = 2 metres
1 *sen* = 40 metres
25 *sen* = 1 kilometre
1 *yot* = 16 kilometres

TWENTY RICHEST THAIS
• • • • • • •

Name	Net worth (in US$)	Age	Marital status	Key source of wealth
1. Dhanin Chearavanont and family	$9 billion	73	married, 5 children	CP Group
2. Chirathivat family	$6.9 billion	n/a	n/a	Central Group
3. Charoen Sirivadhanabhakdi	$6.2 billion	68	married, 5 children	ThaiBev
4. Yoovidhya family	$5.4 billion	n/a	n/a	Red Bull
5. Krit Ratanarak	$3.1 billion	66	divorced, 1 child	Bangkok Broadcasting and Television Company
6. Chamnong Bhirombhakdi	$2.4 billion	84	married, 3 children	Boon Rawd Brewery
7. Vichai Maleenont and family	$1.8 billion	94	widowed, 8 children	BEC World
8. Aloke Lohia	$1.6 billion	53	married, 3 children	Indorama Ventures
9. Prasert Prasarttong-Osoth	$1.2 billion	79	married, 5 children	Bangkok Dusit Medical Service
10. Vanich Chaiyawan and family	$1.16 billion	80	married, 3 children	Thai Life Insurance
11. Thongma Vijitpongpun	$1.1 billion	54	married, 1 child	Pruksa Real Estate
12. Isara Vongkusolkit and family	$1 billion	64	married, 4 children	Mitr Phol Sugar
13. Boonchai Bencharongkul and family	$990 million	58	married, 3 children	Total Access Communications
14. Praneetsilpa Vacharaphol and family	$950 million	80	widowed, 4 children	*Thai Rath* newspaper
15. Surang Prempree	$930 million	70	married	Bangkok Broadcasting and Television Company
16. Prayudh Mahagitsiri and family	$915 million	66	married, 3 children	Quality Coffee
17. Phornthep Phornprapha	$900 million	n/a	married, 3 children	Siam Motors
18. Anant Asavabhokin	$840 million	62	married, 3 children	Lands and Houses
19. Keeree Kanjanapas	$810 million	62	married, 2 children	BTS Group
20. Winai Thongthan	$670 million	n/a	married	Bangkok Dusit Medical Service

Source: *Forbes* magazine; age and marital status as of August 2012.

HOW TO MAKE A NEW PROVINCE
· · · · · · ·

The criteria for establishing a new province was formulated in 1981 by the Cabinet and is still in use today. A district is eligible to become a new province if:

- the new province can be divided into 8 *amphoe* (districts)
- the population of the new province will exceed 300,000 people
- the new province will feature the necessary and proper institutions to administer its affairs
- the majority of the population consents to the idea

Thailand currently has 77 provinces. Prior to 1972, Thailand had 70 provinces. Yasothon was added followed by Payao as the 71st and 72nd provinces respectively. In 1982, Mukdahan became the 73rd province, followed by Sa Kaeo (74th), Nong Bua Lum Phu (75th) and Amnat Charoen (76th), all in 1996. The latest and 77th province, Bueng Kan, was established in 2011.

Source: *Matichon* newspaper

COMPUTER AND INTERNET USAGE
· · · · · · ·

Number of computer users in 2010 (respondents were able to choose multiple answers):

Total number of computer users	At home	At work	At school	In internet cafés	At telecentres	Neighbour
19.1 million	9.3 million	5 million	10.1 million	1.8 million	68,000	404,000

The main objectives for using the internet included:

information search 89%

sending and receiving e-mail 70%

contact with public agencies 9%

customer service 31%

online business 3%

banking and financial services 10%

Sources: National Statistical Office, Ministry of Information and Communication Technology

THE ORIGINAL SIAMESE TWINS
• • • • • • •

The conjoined twins Eng and Chan were born in 1811 in Samut Songkram province. In 1824, Robert Hunter, an English trader saw them swimming in a river. Famous American missionary, Dr Dan Beach Bradley, gave the following account of that first encounter: "It was a creature that appeared to have two heads, four arms, and four legs, all of which were moving in perfect harmony. As Mr Hunter watched, the object climbed into a nearby boat, and to his amazement he realised that he had been looking at two small boys who were joined together at the chest." The twins were born with their livers fused but a later study found that they both functioned independently. Modern technology would have easily separated them.

Hunter took the two boys in 1829 to perform in P.T. Barnum's circus in the United States and Europe as the "Siamese twins". (In Siam, they had been called the "Chinese twins" due to their Chinese heritage.) In 1839, they settled in North Carolina with the intention of living normal lives; they bought slaves and successfully managed a tobacco plantation. They adopted the last name "Bunker" and became American citizens. They married the Yates sisters, Sarah and Adelaide. After sharing the same bed for a time, the two women eventually lived in separate houses and the twins split their time between the two. Eng and Sarah had 11 children. Chan and Adelaide had 10.

In 1874, Chan contracted pneumonia and died. Waking up to find his dead brother, Eng refused any attempt to save his life and died a couple of hours later. Their fused livers are kept at Mutter Museum in Philadelphia. In 2011, more than 200 of their descendants reunited in North Carolina for the 200th birthday of the twins.

HIGHER EDUCATION
• • • • • • •

When Thailand's higher education system is compared to other systems around the world, it does not fare too well. A recent survey compiled for Universitas 21 by researchers at the University of Melbourne used 20 measurements to rank the university systems of 48 nations. Thailand came in 41st place, ahead of India and Indonesia, but behind China and Malaysia. Regionally, Singapore, which was ranked 11th, did the best. The countries with the best university systems, according to the survey, are the United States, Sweden, Canada, Finland and Denmark.

Source: www.universitas21.com

NOT EVERYTHING GOES IN MUAY THAI
· · · · · · ·

Muay Thai is Thailand's national sport and increasingly popular around the world. The sport has many rules and regulations, which may differ slightly depending on the weight class. Common actions considered a foul include:

- Head-butting
- Striking the groin
- Attacking the lower back or spine with either a knee or elbow blow
- Striking another fighter when he is already down. A fighter is considered down when any part of his body except his feet are touching the canvas.
- Pushing, shoving, or wrestling another fighter out of the ring
- Fighting after the referee's command of *yak* (break)
- Fighting after the bell is sounded
- Holding the ropes
- Falling down without being hit
- Using abusive language
- Intentionally evading contact
- Any shoulder, stomach or hip throw
- Dropping one's mouthpiece intentionally
- Foot sweeps
- Using the thumb to the eye

Any of these actions can initiate a warning, followed by deduction of points, and then disqualification.

THE VEGETARIAN FESTIVAL
· · · · · · ·

O ne of the biggest "vegetarian" festivals in the world occurs on the Thai island of Phuket, although the name is a bit of a misnomer in English. In Thai, this festival is usually called *tetsakan/prapheni thue sin kin phak*, which translates literally as "festival/tradition to observe religious precepts and eat vegetables".

The festival is believed to have originated in the early 19th century out of Phuket's community of Hokkien tin miners, who had immigrated from Fujian province in China. Celebrated annually between the first and the ninth day of the ninth month of the Chinese lunar calendar, the festival usually falls in October. Not all vegetables can be consumed during the festival. Five kinds known for their pungent smell are prohibited: garlic, onions (including shallots and spring onion), chives, Chinese garlic and tobacco leaves. In addition to eating a vegetarian diet, there are five other protocols: avoid foods with strong flavours (too spicy, sour or salty), observe the five Buddhist precepts, keep one's mind pure and remain emotionally balanced, give alms and wear white.

ITALIAN ARTISTS IN THE SIAMESE COURT
· · · · · · ·

W hen King Chulalongkorn made a royal visit to Europe in 1897, he was impressed by the Italian art and artists he encountered on his travels, so he hired Casare Ferro as the first Siamese court painter in 1904. Other Italian artists followed, leaving behind a wealth of magnificent paintings, sculptures and architecture, many of which remain major landmarks.

Artist	Years active	Significant works
Mario Tamango	1900–1925	Makawan Bridge, Ambhara Mansion, Wat Benjamaborpit
Casare Ferro	1904–1907	Mural paintings and frescoes at Ambhara Mansion
Annibale Rigotti	1907–1924	Ananta Samakhom Throne Hall
Ercole Manfredi (aka Ekarit Manfredi)	1909–1972	Entrance gate of Chitralada Villa
Carlo Rigoli	1910–1940s	Frescoes and mural paintings at Wat Rachathiwat, Barom Bhiman Mansion and Ananta Samakom Throne Hall
Galileo Chini	1911–1932	Frescoes at Ananata Samakhom Throne Hall
Corrado Feroci (aka Silpa Bhirasri)	1923–1962	Sculptures of King Taksin, King Yodfa (Rama I), King Chulalongkorn and King Vajiravudh; Democracy Monument; Victory Monument and founder of Silpakorn University

Source: *Italians at the Court of Siam* by Leopoldo Ferri de Lazala and Paolo Piazzardi

FOREIGNERS WITH THAI NAMES
· · · · · · ·

S ome foreigners who have contributed to the development of Thailand have been bestowed with Thai names. Some well-known examples:

Original name	Nationality	Thai name	Contribution
Constantine Phaulkon	Greek	*Chao Phraya Vichayen*	Counsellor of King Narai of Ayudhya
Sheikh Ahmad	Iranian	*Chao Phraya Bavorn Rajanayok*	First chief of Muslims during the reign of King Songtham of Ayudhya
Peter Feit	German	*Phra Chen Duriyang*	Composer of the music for the Thai national anthem
William Alfred Goone Tilleke	Sri Lankan	*Phraya Atthakarn Prasit*	Director of the Attorney General during the reign of King Chulalongkorn
Francis Bowes Sayre Sr.	American	*Phraya Kalayana Maitri*	Foreign affairs advisor during the reign of King Vajiravudh
Corrado Feroci	Italian	*Silpa Bhirasri*	Founder of Silapakorn University and considered a pioneer of modern art in Thailand

TAKE THE LONG WAY
· · · · · · ·

- The longest river is the Chi River (765 km). This sleepy river forms in the Petchabun mountain range and runs through several northeastern provinces before joining the Mun river in Ubon Ratchathani province.
- The longest road is Petchkasem road (1,274 km). Also known as Route 4, this southern highway begins in the capital district of Bangkok Yai and passes through more than 10 provinces before reaching the border with Malaysia.
- The longest bridge is Tinsulanonda Bridge (2.64 km). Built in the 1980s and named after the former prime minister, this concrete bridge connects his home province of Songkhla to the nearby island of Koh Yor.
- The longest railroad is the Southern railroad (1,144 km), which connects Bangkok to the southern hub of Hat Yai and ends in Narathiwat.
- The longest mountain range is Thanon Thong Chai mountain range (880 km) stretching from Mae Hong Son province in the north to Kanchanaburi province. Its tallest peak is Doi Inthanon, the highest point in Thailand (of 2,565 metres).
- The longest train tunnel is Khun Tan tunnel (1.35 km). On the northern railway line, this tunnel passes through the Khun Tan range at the border of Lampang and Lamphun provinces.

YOUNG LOVE
· · · · · · ·

S tudies have found that mobile phones and other digital platforms have become one of the main means by which Thai youth profess their love. A recent survey conducted by the Mental Health Department at Rajanagarindra Institute states that the most popular methods are: texting (62%), in person (52%), Hi 5 website (42%), MSN (38%), email (32%) and Facebook (15%). The survey also found that 73% of youths polled believed that the romantic messages might lead to sex.

SOME FILMS BANNED BY THE CENSORS
· · · · · · ·

A ccording to the National Board of Film and Video, a film or video may be banned if it contains content or scenes that are against social order, collective morality, or negatively impact national security or dignity. Some films that have been banned from distribution in Thailand include:

Year	Title	Origin	Reason
1976	*In the Realm of Sense*	Japan	obscenity
1998	*Xiu Xiu: The Sent Down Girl*	China	explicit sexual content
1999	*Anna and the King*	US	disrespectful to the Thai monarchy
2000	*Baise Moi*	France	violence
2006	*Syndromes and a Century*	Thailand	deemed disrespectful to Buddhism and the medical profession
2007	*Halloween*	US	violence
2008	*Zack and Miri Make A Porno*	US	explicit sexual content
2010	*Saw VI*	US	violence
2010	*Insects in the Backyard*	Thailand	deemed immoral and pornographic
2012	*Shakespeare Must Die*	Thailand	deemed as potentially causing disunity among the people due to the film's alleged political connotations

Source: Ministry of Culture

GRADUATION GOWNS

. . . .

Quite like the prom raises a hoo-ha in the US, a graduation is one of the most celebrated occasions in Thai culture. Families come together and dress in their finest, endless photos are taken, and female graduates, in particular, are expected to look their best—some pay for a professional make-up artist or photographer.

Only a few of the graduation gowns in Thailand are iconic and distinguishable at first glance.

Chulalongkorn University:

- Long-sleeved translucent white gown worn over uniform
- Sleeves and hems feature gold and another coloured thread signifying one's faculty
- Two *prakiaw* (Thai coronet) pins on the chest. The *prakiaw* is the university's symbol.

Thammasat University:

- Long-sleeved black gown
- Colour strap held in place by a *dhammachakra* (Wheel of Law) pin, which is the university's symbol; the strap colour signifies the person's faculty
- Soft, white *faux* fur at the end of the strap indicates the degree level, with one layer of fur for a bachelor, two for a master's degree and three for a doctorate

Mahidol University:

- Black gown with coloured collar signifying the faculty
- Blue bow tie
- Western-style graduation cap

Assumption University (ABAC):

- Black gown with coloured collar signifying one's faculty; the collar drops down the front and back of the gown
- Two ABAC logo pins
- Western-style graduation cap

THE ROYAL GAZETTE
· · · · · · ·

The first *Royal Gazette* was published and distributed for free in 1858 during the reign of King Mongkut. The Royal Command announcing the first *Royal Gazette* said the publication was needed because "forged documents, under [royal] seal and notices, are sometimes manufactured by the unscrupulous in the name of His Majesty … as instruments of unjust extortion, thereby causing popular grievances as well as the loss of prestige on the part of the king …"

By 1874 during the reign of King Chulalongkorn, the *Royal Gazette* was published weekly with an annual subscription costing eight baht. It reported official promotions, appointments among the Buddhist clergy, significant births and deaths, and included weather information for farmers. Some foreign news was also included. Today, the *Royal Gazette* is published by the Office of the Prime Minister. Laws are only in effect after being printed there, and it is a particularly valuable source for Thai and international investors, lawyers, consultants, and others, for updates about laws, taxes, stock market rules, requirements for bidding on government contracts and other business-related information.

THE SIKH COMMUNITY
· · · · · · ·

There are approximately 70,000 Sikhs in Thailand. Although that represents only 0.1% of the country's total population, many play prominent roles in the country's cultural and business affairs. Kirpa Ram Madan, the first Sikh to visit Thailand, was a wealthy trader and his gift of an Arabian horse to King Chulalongkorn was warmly received by the king. He later brought his relatives to Thailand and settled. Their descendents, with family names Madan, Narula and Chawla, have become fixtures in Thai society. Today, there are 17 Sikh gurdwaras (temples). One interesting aside: Sikhs and Buddhist monks are the only people who are not required by law to wear helmets when riding a motorcycle.

1884 – Kirpa Ram Madan was the first Sikh to visit Thailand; after arriving from India, he was granted an audience with King Chulalongkorn

1890 – Ladha Singh was the first Sikh to emigrate from India

1905 – Ishar Singh was the first Sikh to travel from India to Chiang Mai, arriving via Burma

1907 – Chiang Mai's first gurdwara, or Sikh temple, was erected

1912 – Bangkok's first gurdwara was built in the Baan Moh neighbourhood

Sources: sikhwiki, *Encyclopaedia Of Southeast Asia And Its Tribes*, American Women's Club of Thailand

WHEN THAILAND PLAYED THE "DREAM TEAM"
·······

I n the 1956 Summer Olympic Games in Melbourne, Australia, Thailand faced off against the
United States in basketball and lost by 72 points (101 to 29). The collegiate star Bill Russell
(who later became one of the all-time greats in the sport) scored 8 points in limited playing
time for the Americans. The victory was the first time any team had scored over 100 points in
Olympic competition and it was also the most lopsided win ever by the US (that margin was
surpassed in 2012 when the US beat Nigeria by 83 points, 156 to 73). For the Thais, well, it was
the last time the country sent a basketball team to the Olympics. The US went on to win the
gold medal. Thailand finished 0–7, averaging 47.3 points per game, while allowing 77.

The scorers for the two teams in the 1956 game:

United States		Thailand	
Ron Tomsic	15 points	Kirindr Chatvalwong	10 points
Bob Jeangerard	13 points	Kuang Saitang	6 points
Chuck Darling	12 points	Suragit Rukpanich	4 points
Jim Walsh	12 points	Mongkol Ounalulom	3 points
K.C. Jones	10 points	Chalaw Sonthong	3 points
Billy Evans	8 points	Chantra Sailee	2 points
Bill Hougland	8 points	Visit Chivacharern	1 point
Bill Russell	8 points	**Total**	**29 points**
Dick Boushka	6 points		
Gib Ford	5 points		
Burdie Haldorson	4 points		
Total	**101 points**		

Sources: www.basketball-reference.com, *Chronicle of Thailand: Headline News Since 1946*

MAKING A NAME FOR ONESELF
·······

I n 1913, Thais became legally required to have last names, as regulated by The Family Name
Act of that year. Previously, Thais were commonly known by only a single given name. In
1962, a new Family Name Act was created, setting the key guidelines that remain to this day.
Among the provisions are:

• The first and last name must not be similar to the King or Queen's names or any royal title,
  and should not be impolite.
• The last name cannot be the same as others registered before it, though exceptions occur.
  This provision means that two people with the same last name are almost certainly related.
• The last name cannot have more than 10 consonants.

ARE THAIS HARD WORKERS?
· · · · · · ·

R esearch by the International Labour Organization published in 2010 shows that the average work week for a Thai is 46.7 hours. In the manufacturing sector, the average is 59.3 hours per week. A selection of the averages for different countries by gender:

Country	Men	Women
Thailand	50.1	42.3
Sri Lanka	29.5	16.1
Korea	61.1	48.8
Indonesia	53.6	40.4
Macao	43.4	40.2

Source: "Working Time Around the World: Trends in working hours, laws, and policies in a global comparative perspective"

THE INFAMOUS MAE CHAMOY
· · · · · · ·

I n the mid-1980s, the Mae Chamoy chit fund scandal rattled the country. Since 1968, the Petroleum Authority of Thailand employee Chamoy Thipso, known widely as Mae Chamoy, had attracted investors to her "oil share" offer with unusually high rates of return. But in 1984, the pyramid scheme collapsed. Some facts from the famous case:

- 16,231 – the number of clients Mae Chamoy drew to the fund
- 4,544,582,440 baht – the amount of money circulated in the fund
- 80,000 pages – the length of the police report on the case
- 186 pages – the length of the handwritten verdict delivered by the judges
- 23,519 – the number of offences Mae Chamoy committed
- 154,005 years – the number of years Mae Chamoy and each of her accomplices were sentenced to (if terms were consecutive)
- 20 years – the actual sentence Mae Chamoy was ordered to serve. The law allowed 20 years as the maximum sentence for fraud
- 7 years, 11 months and 5 days – the actual time Mae Chamoy served of her sentence

Source: Thai State Attorney Museum

TRADITIONAL INSULTS
· · · · · ·

Insult	Translation	Meaning
Tao hua ngu	An old man with a snake behind his head	A tricky old man who likes to seduce young women
Nok song hua	Two–headed bird	A person characterised by duplicity
Lin song chak	Double-tipped tongue	A person whose words can't be trusted
Pak wan kon priaw	Sweet and sour lips	A person who is insincere
Ling lok chao	A monkey who tricks the leader	A young person who mocks an older person behind his back
Wua luem tin	An ox who forgets his own feet	A person who becomes successful and then forgets his roots
Kang kok kuen wor	A toad on a palanquin	A person who reaches a high status and then forgets his roots
Chao mai mi san	A wandering spirit	A person who cannot settle anywhere permanently
Ma huang kang	A dog who is possessive of a fish bone	A person who is possessive about something that he does not even own
Hua lan dai wi	A bald man with a comb	A person who has something that is not useful

MEALS ON WHEELS
• • • • • • •

Khao kaeng (rice and curry) – These vendors offer a variety of ready-made, homestyle Thai dishes. Customers choose to top steamed white rice with any of the available options. The menu typically features curries, stir-fried vegetables, fried eggs and other common dishes.

Ahaan tam sang (made-to-order dishes) – Vendors cook on the spot any common recipe such as fried rice or fried noodles.

Noodles and soups – Sometimes a choice of meat is available, but most street vendors stick to one speciality. Different kinds of noodles can typically be ordered *hang* (without soup), *nam* (with soup) or *kao lao* (without noodles—just the soup and meat). Some beef and pork noodle dishes are made *nam tok* (with a thick soup) by mixing ox or pig blood into the soup.

Isaan food stalls – Northeastern Thai dishes include various kinds of *som tam* (papaya salad) and grilled dishes such as *moo yang* (grilled pork), *kai yang* (grilled chicken), *pla pao* (grilled fish), as well as *nam tok* (spicy salad which can feature pork, chicken or beef), *larb* (spicy salad with minced chicken, pork, duck or fish), *tom sab* (hot and spicy soup), and *sup nor mai* (bamboo shoot salad). All dishes can be eaten with *khao niew* (sticky rice or steamed glutinous rice).

Barbecue stalls – With only one small barbecue grill, these vendors usually sell *moo ping* (grilled pork on a stick) or *kai ping* (grilled chicken on a stick) or both (and sometimes with entrails). These grilled meats are usually accompanied by sticky rice.

Everything deep-fried – A stall with a pan full of boiling oil may offer deep fried snacks like *pueak tod* (deep-fried taro), *tao hu tod* (deep-fried tofu), *khao pod tod* (deep-fried corn), or *hua chai tao tod* (deep-fried turnip). These four usually come together and are served with a sweet and spicy sauce with crushed peanuts. Similar-sized stalls sell other deep-fried snacks such as *sai krok tod* (deep-fried sausage), *kiew tod* (deep-fried wanton) or many types of *luk chin tod* (deep-fried meatballs).

Ice cream trolleys – Ice cream trolleys can offer popsicles and other treats from big global brands or just some old-school coconut ice cream. The latter offers *i-tim kathi* (coconut ice cream) in a cup or a bun, to which toppings can be added, such as *kao niew* (sticky rice), *tua* (peanuts), *luk chit* (palm candy) and *fak thong* (sweet pumpkin).

Fruit trolleys – Already peeled fruits sit on ice. Once the customer orders, the vendor will chop the fruit into pieces and offer it with *prik kub kluer* (a combination of salt, sugar, and chilli).

Tea and coffee – Tea and coffee are available with other beverages such as soda or simple fruit juices. The vendor makes the drinks on the spot.

THE LAST DAY OF THE TRAMS
••••••

Eyewitness account of the last day of the Bangkok trams, on 1 October 1968, by American Paul Gawkowski:

"I was present on the last day of operation of the Bangkok trams on Sunday, 1 October 1968. At the time, I was stationed with the US Army in Korat. I had visited and photographed both remaining sections of the City Circle line shortly after my arrival in Thailand in July.

I was utterly captivated by the tiny yellow and red trams ... The single track operation along the curbs of the street past some of Bangkok's major tourist attractions and the somewhat bemused friendliness of the two-man crews were fascinating and thoroughly enjoyable. At the end of the line, while the motorman moved the trolley pole around the car, the conductor would move two long cushions from one end of the car to the other. The cushions, which were always moved to the front of the car, constituted first class. The fare was 50 satang (2.5 US cents). The rear half of the little tram, with its now bare wooden longitudinal seats, was second class with a 25 satang fare.

When I learned to my dismay that the trams would be abandoned, I wrote letters to the *Bangkok World* and the *Bangkok Post* urging that the trams be retained as a tourist attraction, like the San Francisco cable cars. I also made plans to go to Bangkok on the last day of operation.

On that Sunday, the trams operated normally. The trams were crowded as they ran along the short private right of way near the Sunday Market (Sanam Luang I think), adjacent to the Royal Palace grounds if I remember correctly. Passengers with bundles and baskets from the market packed the open platforms of the little trams. I rode the trams and took more slides and photographs. In the late afternoon, I rode one of the trams back to the car house where the crews, who seemed elderly to a 24-year-old army lieutenant, were having a farewell party. There was Thai food, Singha Beer and Mekong Whiskey. In spite of the language barrier, the ever-hospitable Thai motormen, conductors and other MEA employees invited me to join them. It was a memorable though bittersweet occasion. Aside from the farewell party at the car house, there seemed to be no ceremony to mark the closure of the trams. And, as far as I know, I was the only *farang* to witness their final passage into history ..."

Source: www.2bangkok.com

SOME FAMOUS AND INFAMOUS GOVERNMENT PROJECTS
• • • • • • •

Banning Opium
In 1959, the government of Sarit Thanarat successfully imposed laws banning opium smoking. More than 8,000 opium pipes were set alight in a public display. More than 90 opium dens in Bangkok and Thonburi were shut down, together with more than 1,000 upcountry. Today, opium can still be found in Thailand but abuse of the drug is not very widespread.

Amnesty Offer for Communists
Deciding to shift its focus from suppression of communism to tackling poverty, in 1982, Prem Tinsulanonda's government offered amnesty to members of the Communist Party who laid down their arms. The programme was widely hailed a success as thousands of members of the Communist Party surrendered, ending decades of intermittent fighting.

Smoking Ban in Public
In 1991, during the first premiership of Anand Panyarachun, the Bangkok Metropolitan Administration introduced a ban on smoking in public areas such as public parks, cinemas, buses, schools, hospitals, and some other indoor spaces.

30-Baht Healthcare Scheme
In 2001, Thaksin Shinawatra's government introduced the 30-baht (per visit) universal healthcare scheme to provide medical services for those with no health insurance or social security.

One Tambon, One Product (OTOP)
In 2002, the government of Thaksin Shinawatra implemented this project to encourage people in each sub-district to create a signature local product for both the domestic market and export.

War on Drugs
In 2003, Thaksin Shinawatra announced his government's plan to completely eradicate drugs within three months. Provincial governors and police chiefs were rewarded when they reached the target number of arrests and seizures while those who failed were likely to be sacked. The so-called "War on Drugs" became controversial, with human rights groups decrying extra-judicial killings of drug dealers and users.

Minimum Wage Hike
In 2012, Yingluck Shinawatra's government promised to raise the minimum wage to 300 baht per day (from between 215 and 221 baht), effective in seven pilot provinces (Bangkok, Nonthaburi, Samut Prakarn, Samut Songkram, Nakhon Pathom and Phuket). Workers across the entire country are set to receive the wage hike in 2013.

FOREIGN WRITERS ON BANGKOK
· · · · · · ·

"The general appearance of Bangkok is that of a large primitive village, situated in and mostly concealed by a virgin forest of almost impenetrable density."
–Frank Vincent, *The Land of the White Elephant* (1873)

"There it was, spread largely on both banks, the Oriental capital which has as yet suffered no white conqueror; an expanse of brown houses of bamboo, of mats, of leaves, of a vegetable-matter style of architecture, sprung out of the brown soil on the banks of the muddy river. It was amazing to think that in those miles and miles of human habitations there was not probably half a dozen pounds of nails."
–Joseph Conrad, *The Shadow Line* (1916)

"They are unlike anything in the world, so that you are taken aback, and you cannot fit them into the scheme of the things you know. It makes you laugh with delight to think that anything so fantastic could exist on this somber earth. They are gorgeous; they glitter with gold and whitewash, yet are not garish; against that vivid sky, in that dazzling sunlight, they hold their own, defying the brilliancy of nature and supplementing it with ingenuity and the bold playfulness of man."
–Somerset Maugham, *The Gentleman in the Parlour* (1935), describing Bangkok's temples

"In seedy and improvident Manila, the bars were the fact-buck stuff of a Puritan's nightmare; while in high-tech and prosperous Bangkok, they were quicksilver riddles, less alarming for their sleaze than for their cunning refinement, embellished by the country's exquisite sense of design, softened by the ease of Buddhism, invigorated by the culture of *sanuk* (fun). In Manila girls tried to sell themselves out of sheer desperation; in Bangkok, the crystal palaces of sex were only extra adornments in a bejeweled city that already glittered with ambiguities …"
–Pico Iyer, *Video Night in Kathmandu* (1988)

COMMON TOPPINGS PUT ON COCONUT ICE CREAM
· · · · · · ·

- Roasted peanuts
- Sticky rice
- Taro
- Sweet potato
- Corn kernels
- Water chestnuts
- Pumpkin
- Jackfruit
- Soybeans
- Golden mung beans
- Sweetened pineapple
- Red beans
- Palm candy
- Sweetened star gooseberry
- Raisins

THE IDEAL SIAMESE CAT
· · · · · · ·

Standard breeds of Siamese cats, according to the Traditional Cat Association, should have the following characteristics:

Ears – medium ears with broad bases and round tips, set as much on the side of the head as the top

Eyes – almond-shaped, uncrossed and deep vivid blue

Body – medium to large in size, solidly built, muscular in development, well proportioned, and solid in appearance

Body colour – even with subtle shading (an allowance is made for lighter body colour in young cats and darker colour in older ones)

Tail – medium in length, in proportion to the body, tapered and straight (no kinks)

Head – rounded with a clearly defined muzzle that follows the rounded contour of the head

Nose – slight and gentle dip at eye level

Coat – short but thick enough to have body, satiny and somewhat close-lying, but not tight or flat, plush and soft in texture, resilient and firm to the touch

Legs – muscular, length and bone in proportion

Paws – more round than oval

Source: *The Legend of Siamese Cats* by Martin Clutterbuck

THE PALACE LAW OF SUCCESSION, SECTION 11
· · · · · · ·

Section 11 of The Palace Law of Succession states: "Descendants of the royal family with any of the following characteristics shall be excluded from the line of succession:

1. Insanity;
2. Convicted of a serious crime;
3. Unable to serve as Upholder of Buddhism;
4. Married to a foreign consort, i.e. a woman whose nationality is originally not Thai;
5. Being removed from the position of heir to the throne regardless of during which reign such removal took place;
6. Being proclaimed to be excluded from the line of succession."

A WAR OF WORDS
· · · · · · ·

On the morning of 24 June 1932, a group of military officers and civilians calling themselves the People's Party staged a coup against the throne. They commandeered military vehicles and tanks in the capital and detained key members of the military and royal members. They also distributed a deliberately provocative leaflet attacking the monarch, King Prajadhipok:

> *When the present king succeeded his brother to the throne, some people at first expected him to rule with justice for the good of his subjects. Their hopes did not materialise. The king was above the law as before … He rules without any guiding principle. As a result the destiny of the nation was left at random, as evidenced by economic depression and the misery and hardship of the people, which is generally known. The absolute monarchy was unable to remedy these wrongs … The king's government rules dishonestly with deception. It has made the people believe it would promote their economic wellbeing. But the people have waited in vain.*

Soon after, King Prajadhipok signed a preliminary constitution, which turned Siam into a constitutional monarchy, ending his absolute rule. However, over time, King Prajadhipok became frustrated with the People's Party's hostility. On 2 March 1935, while residing in England, King Prajadhipok abdicated. A part of his abdication statement reads:

> *I am willing to surrender the powers I formerly exercised to the people as a whole, but I am not willing to turn them over to any specific individual or any group to use them in an autocratic manner without heeding the voice of the people.*

Source: *King Bhumibol Adulyadej: A Life's Work*

KEEP OFF THE GRASS, HIPPIES!
· · · · · · ·

On 27 June 1980, the *Bangkok Post* newspaper reported on a new push by the immigration police aimed at denying entry to any travellers who looked like "hippies". Officials were told hippies could be identified by these characteristic traits or fashion choices:

- a singlet or waistcoat with no vest
- shorts worn "in an impolite manner"
- slippers
- silk trousers
- long and untidy hair
- a dirty-looking appearance

NAGA FIREBALLS
·······

The strange phenomenon on the Mekong River known as the Naga fireballs (*bang fai phaya nak*) have long been shrouded in myth and remain unexplained by science. The fireballs, which have been spotted along a 100-kilometre stretch of the Mekong in Nong Khai province as long as anyone can remember, typically appear only on the last night of Buddhist Lent (*ok pansa*) in October, though some people claim to see them on other nights. The sight now attracts thousands of revellers who cheer them as they shoot up from the river. "The lights looked a bit like exploding flares," described *Time* magazine correspondent Jason Gagliardi, "though there was no hiss or smoke, no sparkling arc back to earth. To a cynic like myself, they looked indisputably man-made. But to the believers—gathered in the tens of thousands along the riverbank—this was the breath of the Naga, the mythical serpent of Buddhist lore that many Thais believe haunts the broad reaches of the Mekong in Nong Khai province." Indeed, while some scientists believe (and others dispute) that the fireballs are the result of the ignition of pockets of methane gas in the riverbed, locals are adamant that the fiery orbs are proof that the Naga calls this stretch of the Mekong home.

GLOBAL PEACE INDEX
·······

The Global Peace Index, produced by the Institute for Economics and Peace, uses 23 qualitative and quantitative indicators measuring civil and international conflict, safety and security in society and the militarisation of countries around the world. Among the Global Peace Index indicators measured are "perceived criminality in society", "homicides", "jailed population", "political terror", "military expenditure" and many more. The sixth edition of this survey was released in 2012, and Thailand scored 126 out of 158 countries, meaning it was one of the least peaceful nations on earth, according to the survey. (In 2011, it ranked 109th out of 153 countries.) Iceland was the most peaceable country while Somalia was the least. The rankings of Thailand and some other nearby countries:

20 – Malaysia
34 – Vietnam
37 – Laos
63 – Indonesia
108 – Cambodia
126 – Thailand
139 – Myanmar

Source: www.visionofhumanity.org

COUP ANYONE?
. . . .

Date	Leader(s)	Result of coup attempt
24 June 1932	General Phraya Phahol Pholphayuhasena (leader of the People's Party)	Ended absolute monarchy and led to formation of constitutional monarchy
20 June 1933	General Phraya Phahol Pholphayuhasena	Took over power from Phraya Manopakornnititthada due to friction within the People's Party
11 October 1933	Prince Bavoradej	Failed to overthrow the government which he accused of being Communist
1 August 1935	Sergeant Major Sawat Mahamad	Failed to overthrow the government
29 January 1938	Phraya Songsuradej	Failed to bring the country back under absolute monarchy
8 November 1947	Pin Choonhavan	Overthrew the government of Rear Admiral Thawal Thamrongnawasawat
6 April 1948	Group of high-ranking army officials	Overthrew the government of Khuang Aphaiwong

TOP TEN POPULATIONS BY PROVINCE
. . . .

1. Bangkok (8.25 million)
2. Nakhon Ratchasima (2.52 million)
3. Samut Prakarn (1.83 million)
4. Ubon Ratchathani (1.74 million)
5. Khon Kaen (1.74 million)
6. Chiang Mai (1.71 million)
7. Chon Buri (1.55 million)
8. Songkhla (1.48 million)
9. Nakhon Si Thammarat (1.45 million)
10. Nonthaburi (1.33 million)

Source: National Statistical Office, 2010 census

1 October 1948	Major General Somboon Saranuchid and Major General Netra Khemayothin	Planned to overthrow the government of Field Marshal Pibul Songgram but was caught before the plan was enacted
26 June 1949	Pridi Banomyong	Failed to overthrow the government of Field Marshal Pibul Songgram
29 June 1951	Captain Anond Buntarikthada	Failed to overthrow the government of Field Marshal Pibul Songgram
29 November 1951	Field Marshal Pibul Songgram	Known as the "silent coup", it was a coup staged by Pibul against his own government to consolidate its existing power
16 September 1957	Field Marshal Sarit Thanarat	Overthrew the government of Field Marshal Pibul Songgram
20 October 1958	Field Marshal Sarit Thanarat	Overthrew the government of Field Marshal Thanom Kittikachorn
17 November 1971	Field Marshal Thanom Kittikachorn	Staged a coup against his own government, which led to the abrogation of the constitution, dissolution of Parliament and disbanding of the Cabinet
6 October 1976	Admiral Sa-ngad Chaloryoo	After a massacre of students and protesters by right-wing groups in Bangkok, the military took control of the government.
26 March 1977	General Chalard Hiranyasiri	Failed to overthrow the government of Thanin Kraivixien and was then executed
20 October 1977	Admiral Sa-ngad Chaloryoo	Overthrew the government of Thanin Kraivixien
1 April 1981	General Sant Chitpatima	Failed to overthrow the government of General Prem Tinsulanonda
9 September 1985	Colonel Manoonkrit Roopkachorn	Failed to overthrow the government of General Prem Tinsulanonda
23 February 1991	General Sunthorn Kongsompong	Overthrew the government of Chatichai Choonhavan
19 September 2006	General Sonthi Boonyaratkalin	Overthrew the government of Thaksin Shinawatra

FAMOUS FOOTPRINTS
• • • • • • •

Three months after Neil Armstrong and Edwin Aldrin Jr landed on the moon in 1969, they arrived in Thailand on their celebratory world tour. As part of the visit, they went to Pattaya (Chon Buri province) and Koh Sak (a nearby island) where the pair left their footprints in cement. Lady Bird Johnson (wife of US President Johnson), the Shah of Iran Reza Pahlavi, the Duke of Edinburgh (Prince Philip) and His Majesty King Bhumibol Adulyadej have also left their footprints there, having all visited when Koh Sak was famous for its turtle sanctuary.

BUYING A NEW LOOK
· · · · · · ·

The market value of the cosmetic surgery business, one of Thailand's fastest growing industries, was 20 billion baht (US$645 million) in 2011, and is expected to rise another 20 percent in 2012. There are 350 plastic surgery clinics registered with the Public Health Ministry. Among teenagers, nose and eyelid surgeries are the most popular procedures. Here are some of the typical costs of common surgeries:

- Buttock augmentation: 150,000 baht
- Cheekbone reduction: 110,000 baht
- Mandible (jaw) angle reduction: 75,000 baht
- Nose reshaping: 65,000 baht
- Tummy tuck: 60,000 baht
- Forehead lift: 60,000 baht
- Chin implant: 33,000 baht
- Adam's apple shaving: 26,000 baht
- Nose implant: 20,000 baht
- Upper or lower blepharoplasty (eyelid reconstruction): 18,000 baht

Sources: *The Nation* newspaper, Yanhee International Hospital

WE ARE THE WORLD HERITAGE SITES
· · · · · · ·

There are two types of sites under the listings of UNESCO World Heritage: cultural and natural. To date, the following categories have been created to classify the different sites: cultural landscapes, historic towns and centres, heritage canals and heritage routes. Some determinants include intelligibility, outstanding universal value, and how illustrative it is of the evolution of human society. To date, Thailand has five sites listed.

- Historic City of Ayutthaya (Cultural site)
- Historic Town of Sukhothai and Associated Historic Towns (Cultural site)
- Thungyai-Huai Kha Khaeng Wildlife Sanctuaries (Natural site)
- Ban Chiang Archaeological Site (Cultural site)
- Dong Phayayen-Khao Yai Forest Complex (Natural site)

Source: UNESCO

THAI FIGURES AT MADAME TUSSAUD'S
· · · · · · ·

The wax museum Madame Tussaud's has branches around the world, including in Bangkok. Some famous Thai figures are represented among the other world celebrities. They are:

- HRH Prince Mahitala Thibed Adulyadej Vikrom Phra Baroma Rajajanok (Prince Mahidol, the King's father)
- HRH Princess Srinagarinda (The Princess Mother)
- Field Marshal Pibul Songgram (Former prime minister)
- *Mom Rajawongse* Seni Pramoj (Founder of Democrat party)
- Buddhadasa Bhikkhu (Revered Buddhist monk)
- General Prem Tinsulanonda (Former prime minister)
- Sunthorn Phu (Legendary poet)
- Dr Porntip Rojanasunan (Pathologist)
- Silpa Bhirasri (Father of modern art in Thailand)
- *Mom Rajawongse* Kukrit Pramoj (National artist and former prime minister)
- Luang Vichit Vadakan (Nationalist leader)
- Khaosai Galaxy (Boxer)
- Pawina Thongsuk (Weightlifter)
- Tata Young (Pop star)
- Ad Carabao (Singer)
- Pumpuang Duangjan (Country singer)
- Yodrak Salakjai (Country singer)
- Bie The Star (Singer)
- Petchara Chaowarat (Actress)
- Mitr Chaibancha (Actor)
- Sombat Metanee (Actor)
- Tony Jaa (Actor)
- Khan Kluay (Animated elephant character)
- "Pancake" Khemanit Jamikorn (Actress)
- Anne Thongprasom (Actress)
- Ken Theeradej Wongpuapan (Actor)

SALARY COMPARISONS

R esearch by an international recruiting agency compared the salary ranges of those holding senior positions (more than five years experience) in different job categories. Some of the results (monthly salaries in baht):

	Accounting	Admin/ Secretarial	Customer Service	Engineering	Engineering Business	Finance
Min	20,000	20,000	25,000	15,000	30,000	35,000
Max	220,000	220,000	80,000	300,000	300,000	200,000

	Human Resources	IT	IT Business	Insurance	Legal Complaints	Logistics
Min	35,000	20,000	50,000	45,000	30,000	40,000
Max	200,000	200,000	200,000	60,000	150,000	60,000

	Marketing/ PR	Medicine/ Science	Sales	Supply Chain	Technical/ Manufacturing	Top Management
Min	25,000	35,000	25,000	20,000	20,000	70,000
Max	180,000	200,000	220,000	130,000	150,000	600,000

Sources: www.2bangkok.com and Adecco's Thailand Salary Guide; data from 2011 and 2012.

YOU ANIMAL, YOU!

I n Thailand, being referred to as a particular animal has negative connotations and implications, as follows:

Monkey .... naughty, mischievous, hyperactive
Buffalo .... stupid
Rhinoceros (for women only) .... saucy, slutty
Monitor lizard .... vile, evil, a contemptible person
Snake (for men only) .... promiscuous
Cockroach (for men only) .... an immoral, disgusting character
Bear (Asian Black Bear) .... big, oversized
Dog .... foul-mouthed, a lowly character or cheat
Pig .... obese

THE RULES OF COCKFIGHTING
• • • • • • •

*C*ockfighting is a traditional Thai spectacle that still takes place at registered premises today. In the past, these competitions usually marked the end of the harvesting season, but today they are essentially a gambling attraction.

Roosters that show strength and bravery will be kept in excellent condition by their owners and will be trained as though they are athletes. During the training period, the cock is washed in the morning and kept away from sunlight. After it dries, it is allowed to rest until its training time in the afternoon, when it is splashed with water again before practising dodging and manoeuvring. A good fighting cock can cost up to 100,000 baht. With the spread of bird flu in the region, (failed) efforts were made to further regulate and even ban cockfighting.

A typical "amateur" fight (not intended for gambling) is four rounds of 10 minutes each. The fight ends one of two ways: by "technical knock-out", when one rooster is not willing to fight anymore after the referee puts the combatants face to face three consecutive times, or by the referee, when he stops the fight because a rooster's beak has fallen off or its eye has been pecked out. In "professional" fights (those regulated for gambling), the fight is up to 12 rounds of 20 minutes each (yes, four hours). The fight is decided when one rooster refuses to continue after being faced off with its opponent three consecutive times.

Source: Cockfight database by Phibulsongkram Rajabhat University

SPIRIT HOUSES
· · · · · · ·

Thais believe that every plot of land is guarded by the spirit of its previous occupant. To appease these spirits and create harmony in the household, spirit houses, or *san phra phum*, are built in an auspicious location on the property. While there is little evidence as to when this practice began, it is believed that some spirit houses existed prior to the Sukhothai era.

Spirit houses are usually miniature versions of houses or temples, and are built using materials such as wood, mortar, marble and glass. These mounted shrines may contain figurines of people or animals, or even small dolls, which represent the guardian spirit, and their servants or horses. Votive offerings of incense, candles, flowers and food are left in these houses as a means of honouring the guardian spirits.

Thais believe that if these spirits are disrespected or angered, the people who dwell on that plot of land could be afflicted by illness or even death.

HOW TO START A SUCCESSFUL SWIFTLET FARM
· · · · · · ·

1. Identify and rent or, preferably, purchase a building that has the potential to be converted into a successful swiftlet farm. The building must be located where there are signs of swiftlet activity and it must not be obstructed by other buildings.

2. Remove the top floor ceiling and put meranti wood plank frames and ceiling boards in place.

3. Mount steel plates on top of the ceiling boards in order to enhance roof stability and security.

4. Erect brick walls on the inside of the front and back windows of the building to prevent break-ins. Make sure that each wall is equipped with numerous ventilation points. Cover the walls with cement.

5. Buy a sound system, install internal and external speakers in your building and broadcast chirping sounds to encourage the swiftlets to visit and reside in your farm.

6. Install a humidifying system to maintain the farm's humidity at around 75–80%.

7. Wait for the swiftlets to come and build their nests. Do not harvest the nests with eggs or hatchlings inside.

Source: *Make Millions from Swiftlet Farming: A Definitive Guide* by Dr Christopher Lim, 2007

A PASSAGE FROM A CLASSIC
• • • • • • •

The Tale of Khun Chang Khun Phaen is a classic of the Thai language. A love story, set against the background of war, and ending in high tragedy, this folk epic was first developed in oral form for popular performance with a fast-paced blend of romance, tragedy, and farce spiced with sex, war, adventure and the supernatural. It was later adopted by the Siamese court and written down, with two kings contributing. This passage, chosen by historian Chris Baker, comes from a recent English translation of the epic by Baker and Pasuk Phongpaichit:

> [*The first meeting of the couple; he's a novice monk and she's giving alms at Songkran*]
>
> Phim devoutly brought bananas, sweets and sharp oranges on a large tray. Carrying a bowl of rice, she walked gracefully to give to the seniors and then down the line.
>
> Coming to Novice Kaeo, she glanced at him and hesitated, remembering something from the past. "This novice and I seem to know each other." She ladled a big scoop of food with a heap of fried pork, dried fish, chicken curry, halved boiled eggs, sausages, dried fish, watermelon, and a bowlful of curry—enough to fill him up.
>
> Novice Kaeo had his head bowed and did not know who it was. Seeing so much food, he lifted his head with eyes opened wide. He saw Phim's face smiling with her eyes averted. "Is she teasing me or what?"
>
> "You're giving me so much my bowl is packed to overflowing. How can I eat it? There's too much, both sweet and savory, but you haven't given me what I really like."
>
> Phim broke into a smile. "Oh Novice, when I saw the empty bowl, I thought it was an old mendicant, so I heaped it in. You accuse me of teasing. Would you rather have me lose merit?"
>
> Phlai Kaeo thought for a moment with his heart thumping. "I can remember. I think she used to play with me. Her name is Phim Philalai. She's grown up so beautiful she makes my eyes hurt."

Source: *The Tale of Khun Chang Khun Phaen* (published by Silkworm Books)

REEL HISTORY
• • • • • • •

The 1923 Universal production directed by Henry MacRae, *Miss Suwanna of Siam* (or *Nangsao Suwan*) was the first film to be shot in Thailand with Thai cast and crew. The film was also shown in America under the title *Kingdom of Heaven*. In 1927, Krungthep Pabpayon Company produced *Chok Song Chan*, the film commonly cited as the first Thai film with an entirely Thai crew and no foreign involvement.

A HISTORY OF SEX, ER ... FAMILY STUDIES
· · · · · · ·

The introduction of sex education in Thailand can be traced back to 1942. At that time, discussing sex was very taboo and few dared mention the topic in public.

1942 – The National Cultural Council started to conduct research on sex education.

1958 – Guidelines for teaching sex education to schoolchildren at every level were completed. However, the Education Ministry decided not to include the guidelines in compulsory education, fearing that Thai students were not yet capable or ready to learn about sex.

1978 – Sex education was finally included in compulsory education. However, the word "sex" was avoided. Instead, euphemisms such as "the natural aspect of life", "individual and family life", or "life and family studies" were used to describe the instruction.

1982 – Sex education was taught as part of the social science, health education and domestic science modules.

1987 – A sex education manual and communication materials were created by the Planned Parenthood Association of Thailand to be used for teaching at the secondary level. The manual is officially called "The Family Studies Manual".

2000 – The Ministry of Public Health started to compile information for a new sex education curriculum.

2002 – The new sex education curriculum by the Ministry of Public Health is officially included in the health education and physical education modules. The curriculum was titled "Life and Family Studies".

Source: *Sexuality in Transition in Thai Society* by Kritaya Archavanitkul

MIND THE LINE: SKYTRAIN STATS
· · · · · · ·

BTS Group Holding Public Company Limited operates Bangkok's elevated "Skytrain" on two lines (Silom and Sukhumvit) with 30 stations (as of August 2012). The cheapest ride is 15 baht while the most expensive is 55 baht. Other key figures:

Total ridership (from December 1999 to May 2012) .... 1.5 billion
Average daily ridership in July 2012 538,998
Total employees 3,045
Book value of total property assets .... 13.7 billion baht
Total annual operating revenue .... 7.86 billion baht
Gross annual operating profit .... 3.86 billion baht

Source: BTS Group Holding Public Company's Annual Report 2011/2012

LONGEST PLACE NAME IN THE WORLD
· · · · · · ·

A mong locals, Bangkok is referred to as *Krung Thep*, or "City of Angels". *Krung Thep* is in fact the shortened version of the world's longest place name as listed in *Guinness World Records*:

Krung Thep Mahanakhon Amon Rattanakosin Mahintharayutthaya Mahadilok Phop Noppharat Ratchathani Burirom Udomratchaniwet Mahasathan Amon Phiman Awatan Sathit Sakkathattiya Witsanukam Prasit

กรุงเทพมหานคร อมรรัตนโกสินทร์
มหินทรายุทธยา มหาดิลกภพ
นพรัตนราชธานีบุรีรมย์
อุดมราชนิเวศน์มหาสถาน
อมรพิมานอวตารสถิต
สักกะทัตติยะวิษณุกรรมประสิทธิ์

This translates as: "City of angels. The great city. The eternal jewel city. The impregnable city of God Indra. The grand capital of the world endowed with nine precious gems, the happy city, abounding in an enormous royal palace that resembles the heavenly abode where reigns the reincarnated god, a city built by Vishnukam, according to Indra's command."

THAI AIRWAYS ROUTE EXPANSION DURING ITS FIRST 25 YEARS
· · · · · · ·

1960 – Inaugural flight to Hong Kong, Taipei and Tokyo in May. Additional services added to Rangoon, Calcutta, Kuala Lumpur, Singapore, Saigon, Phnom Penh, Manila and Jakarta by the end of the year.
1964 – Osaka
1966 – Penang
1967 – Bali
1968 – Seoul; Delhi; Kathmandu
1971 – Sydney (first intercontinental route)
1972 – Copenhagen (first European route)
1973 – London; Frankfurt
1974 – Rome
1975 – Amsterdam; Paris; Athens
1977 – Kuwait
1978 – Bahrain
1980 – Seattle (first US route); Melbourne; Noumea
1981 – Guangzhou
1982 – Brisbane; Perth
1983 – Beijing
1984 – Muscat; Zurich

WHEN TRANSVESTITES MEET THE MILITARY DRAFT
·······

When Thai men reach age 21, they are required by law to enter the military draft. For years, *katoey* (transvestites or transgendered persons) who participated in the draft were summarily dismissed on the basis of "permanent psychological problems".

In 2011, three *katoey* successfully sued the Ministry of Defence, claiming the official classification "tarnished our dignity", according to the plaintiffs. The Ministry agreed to a change, and it now categorises *katoey* as people whose "current sexual condition does not match their gender at birth".

COST OF LIVING IN BANGKOK IN 1942
·······

Cinema ticket at Chalermkrung theatre	24 satang (US 12 cents)
Two duck eggs	3 satang
Black iced coffee	5 satang
Glass of ice water	1 satang
Pad Thai with egg	6 satang
Public toilet fee	1 satang
Monthly rental of a wooden house	15 baht
Monthly salary for a man with a bachelor degree	80 baht
Monthly salary for army or police privates	12 baht
"Short-time" with prostitute	75 satang

Source: Ajin Panjaphan, contributor to www.2bangkok.com; note: 100 satang equals 1 baht.

FUNCTIONS OF THE PRIVY COUNCIL

The origins of the Thai Privy Council date to the reign of King Chulalongkorn. According to section 12 of the 2007 Constitution, the Privy Council's duty is to give "advice to the king on all matters pertaining to his functions". The Privy Council of Thailand currently has 18 members. Privy councillors are appointed for life. As of 2011, the president of the Privy Council makes 121,990 baht a month while other members make 112,250 baht.

According to the Constitution, the Privy Council is routinely commanded by the king to perform the following functions:
- Deliberate and submit its view on all matters in which the government requests the king's signature or sanction, such as legislation, royal decrees or appointment of higher officials
- Consider petitions for clemency from prisoners as well as other petitions submitted by private citizens
- Serve on behalf of the king's initiatives such as on the board of the Anandamahidol Foundation or in service to royally initiated development projects
- Represent the king at special events (for example, laying wreaths at funerals)
- Attend court functions

In addition, under special circumstances, the Privy Council may be called upon to:
- Submit the name of a suitable person to hold the office of regent
- The president of the Privy Council can serve as temporary regent *pro tempore* ("for the time being")
- Draft the palace law amendment
- Submit the name of the successor to the throne in the case that there is no heir designated and the throne becomes vacant

Source: *King Bhumibol Adulyadej: A Life's Work*

ENGLISH-SPEAKING YEAR 2012

The Ministry of Education announced the campaign "English-Speaking Year 2012" to encourage all students at schools to speak English at least three days a week. To comply with this campaign, the Office of Basic Education Commission launched the project, "English Canteen", encouraging schoolchildren to speak English to vendors in the school canteen. The only problem was that the vast majority of canteen vendors could not understand or speak English.

Source: Ministry of Education

A STORY WITH LEGS
· · · · · · ·

W idely believed to be a true story when it was printed in the *Bangkok Post* in May 1967 and subsequently reprinted abroad, Kenneth Langbell's review of a piano recital remains a relatively famous piece of satire.

CHOP CHOP

The recital last evening in the chamber music room of the Erawan Hotel by US pianist Myron Kropp

T he first appearance of Mr Kropp in Bangkok can only be described by this reviewer and those who witnessed Mr Kropp's performance as one of the most interesting experiences in a very long time.

A hush fell over the room as Mr Kropp appeared from the right of the stage, attired in black formal evening-wear with a small white poppy in his lapel. With sparse, sandy hair, a sallow complexion and a deceptively frail looking frame, the man who has re-popularised Johann Sebastian Bach approached the Baldwin Concert Grand, bowed to the audience and placed himself upon the stool.

It might be appropriate to insert at this juncture that many pianists, including Mr Kropp, prefer a bench, maintaining that on a screw-type stool, they sometimes find themselves turning sideways during a particularly expressive strain. There was a slight delay, in fact, as Mr Kropp left the stage briefly, apparently in search of a bench, but returned when informed that there was none.

As I have mentioned on several other occasions, the Baldwin Concert Grand, while basically a fine instrument, needs constant attention, particularly in a climate such as Bangkok. This is even more true when the instrument is as old as the one provided in the chamber music room of the Erawan Hotel. In this humidity, the felts which separate the white keys from the black tend to swell, causing an occasional key to stick, which apparently was the case last evening with the D in the second octave.

During the "raging storm" section of the D-Minor Toccata and Fugue, Mr Kropp must be complimented for putting up with the awkward D. However, by the time the "storm" was past and he had gotten into the Prelude and Fugue in D Major, in which the second octave D plays a major role, Mr Kropp's patience was wearing thin.

Some who attended the performance later questioned whether the awkward key justified some of the language which was heard coming from the stage during softer passages of the fugue. However, one member of the audience, who had sent his children out of the room by the midway point of the fugue, had a valid point when he commented over the music and extemporaneous remarks of Mr Kropp that the workman who had greased the stool might have done better to use some of the grease on the second octave D. Indeed, Mr Kropp's stool had more than enough grease and during one passage in which the music and lyrics were both particularly violent, Mr Kropp was turned completely around. Whereas before his remarks had been aimed largely at the piano and were therefore somewhat muted, to his surprise and that of those in the chamber music room he found himself addressing himself directly to the audience.

But such things do happen, and the person who began to laugh deserves to be severely reprimanded for this undignified behavior. Unfortunately, laughter is contagious, and by the time it had subsided and the audience had regained its composure Mr Kropp appeared somewhat shaken. Nevertheless, he swiveled himself back into position facing the piano and, leaving the D Major Fugue unfinished, commenced on the Fantasia and Fugue in G Minor.

Why the concert grand piano's G key in the third octave chose that particular time to begin sticking I hesitate to guess. However, it is certainly safe to say that Mr Kropp himself did nothing to help matters when he began using his feet to kick the lower portion of the piano instead of operating the pedals as is generally done.

Possibly it was this jarring or the un-Bach-like hammering to which the sticking keyboard was being subjected. Something caused the right front leg of the piano to buckle slightly inward, leaving the entire instrument listing at approximately a 35-degree angle from that which is normal. A gasp went up from the audience, for if the piano had actually fallen, several of Mr Kropp's toes, if not both his feet, would surely have been broken.

It was with a sign of relief therefore that the audience saw Mr Kropp slowly rise from his stool and leave the stage. A few men in the back of the room began clapping and when Mr Kropp reappeared a moment later it seemed he was responding to the ovation. Apparently, however, he had left to get a red-handled fire ax which was hung back stage in case of fire, for that was what was in his hand.

My first reaction at seeing Mr Kropp begin to chop at the left leg of the grand piano was that he was attempting to make it tilt at the same angle as the right leg and thereby correct the list. However, when the weakened legs finally collapsed altogether with a great crash and Mr Kropp continued to chop, it became obvious to all that he had no intention of going on with the concert.

The ushers, who had heard the snapping of piano wires and splintering of sounding board from the dining room, came rushing in and, with the help of the hotel manager, two Indian watchmen and a passing police corporal, finally succeeded in disarming Mr Kropp and dragging him off the stage.

Source: *Bangkok Post*, www.snopes.com

WAT DHAMMAKAYA
• • • • • • •

W at Dhammakaya, a popular temple among devout Buddhists, was established in 1970 by Chandra Khonnokyoong, who was a disciple of the Great Abbot of Wat Paknam.

There are 1,470 monks, 443 novices, 161 laymen and 650 laywomen comprising the temple community. A congregation on Sunday or during major religious holidays can attract more than 100,000 participants to the temple, which is spread over 196 *rai* (around 77.5 acres).

Wat Dhammakaya also has worldwide centres in 27 countries, including in Bahrain, Qatar, United Arab Emirates and South Africa.

Two of the stories told by the abbots of Wat Dhammakaya:

> *The story about the* mae chii *(nuns) of Wat Paknam which flew up to push away the bombs (from dropping on Bangkok) during World War Two … You may ask why the bombs fell on Japan and killed so many people. I can answer by saying the power of the Dhamma pulled them to Japan because the Japanese were bellicose and wanted to make war. That pulled the bombs in their direction.*
> —Story about World War II bombings by Phra Dhattacheewo, the deputy abbot of Dhammakaya

> *The heavenly palace in a spacious land is made of silver and white metal, and a combination of crystal-like material. It is not far away from his house in the human world … In this heavenly palace, he sleeps in a luxurious bed that can float in the air. Whenever he wants to listen to his favourite song, the song will automatically play without any of the electrical equipment needed in the human world.*
> —Story about the afterlife of Steve Jobs, published on the Dhammakaya Media Channel website

Sources: www.dhammakaya.net, www.dmc.tv, *The New Buddhist Movements in Thailand*

CANDY-COLOURED CABS
• • • • • • •

P erhaps Thailand's roads should be called "Rainbow Roads" thanks to the cabs that come in a variety of vivid colours—hot pink, green, orange, bright blue and more. There's actually a meaning to the colours too. A yellow-and-green taxi is owned by the driver. If it is any other colour, that means it is company-owned and that the driver has rented the cab. Different colours correspond to different companies. As of 2012, there were 101,000 registered taxis in the country: 77,000 company-owned cabs and 24,000 privately owned ones.

Source: National Land Transport Department

THE SNIFF KISS
· · · · · · ·

> **"E**skimos rub noses. Westerners join lips. Starlets air-kiss everyone. The French involve first both cheeks, and then the tongue. So how do Thais express amour. They sniff. A light, quick inhalation, somewhere around the cheek, is the acme of endearment. The *hom kaem* (sniff kiss) confirms both unconditional love to one's child and understated passion between lovers."
>
> –Philip Cornwel-Smith, *Very Thai: Everyday Popular Culture*

SEVEN POPULAR COMEDIANS FROM DIFFERENT ERAS
· · · · · · ·

Lor Tok

Nose Udom

Comedian	Career span	Famous for …
Sawong Subsubruay aka Lor Tok	1933–2002	He played a poor man who rises to fame and forgets where he came from in the film *Klai Kuer Kin Kuer*. The name of the character, Lor Tok, became his for life.
Chusri Rojanapradit aka Chusri Meesommon	1942–1992	She had a unique ability to imitate the voices and actions of celebrities; also co-hosted TV programme *Khai Hua Roh* with Lor Tok.
Narong Rataporn aka Krong Kangkengdaeng	1957–2011	This film comedian was famous for always wearing red pants.
Bunpot Veerarat, Somjai Sukjai and Suthep Pho-ngarm aka Den Dokpradu, Der Doksadao and Thep Pho-ngarm	1977–present	One of the first café comedy groups to star in movies.
Udom Taepanich aka Nose Udom	1990–present	First successful standup comedian in Thailand.
Petchtai Wongkamlao aka Mum Jokmok	1992–present	Mum represented "the joker" on the game show *Ching Roi Ching Lan*.
Charoenporn On-Lamai aka Koh Tee Aram Boy	1993–present	His child-like appearance (he suffers from a growth hormone deficiency).

A DOOMED MARRIAGE? PAIRING THAI DISHES WITH WINE
• • • • • • •

Some argue it's impossible. Some say Thai food just doesn't go well with wine. But the wine industry would never admit that about any cuisine. The spicy and sharp flavours of Thai food can certainly overshadow the subtleties of wine, but that doesn't mean you can't enjoy some vintages with your delicious curry.

Dishes	Suggested wines
Grilled beef, pork or chicken	Pinot Gris, Chenin Blanc, dry rosé or dry Lambrusco
Som tam (green papaya salad), *yum nuea* (spicy beef salad), *larb moo/kai* (spicy northeastern-style pork or chicken salad), *tom yum* (spicy and sour soup) or *tom ka* (spicy soup with coconut milk)	Torrontés, Alvarinho, dry Viognier or Sauvignon Blanc
Fish cakes, fried or grilled fish served with *nam pla* (fish sauce)	Dry Muscat, Gewurztraminer or Edelzwicker
Pad Thai (fried noodles)	Riesling, Scheurebe, Pinot Gris or Zinfandel
Kuay tiew pad (stir-fried noodles) or *khao pad* (fried rice)	Dry Riesling, any sparkling wine or sherry-like wine, Barbera, Merlot
Panang (red curry) or *massaman* (yellow curry)	White wines from Alsace or the Anderson Valley, Riesling, Merlot or Lambrusco

Source: *The Chronicle Pairing Guide*

THE WHEEL OF LAW
• • • • • • •

The Wheel of Law, or *dhammachakra*, symbolises the Buddha's teachings on the cycle of life and points the way toward enlightenment. It is one of the oldest and best-known symbols of the religion, originating under the Indian emperor Ashoka, and it usually features eight spokes that represent the Noble Eightfold Path. The Buddha proposed a way to end suffering and attain *nirvana* by practising correct thought, correct speech, correct actions, correct livelihood, correct understanding, correct effort, correct mindfulness and correct concentration.

In Thailand, the *dhammachakra* is featured on the country's Buddhist flag as well as on the seal of the country's second oldest university, Thammasat University (the symbol represents the university's commitment to Buddhist principles).

THE SOCIAL NETWORK
· · · · · · ·

General statistics:
- Number of Thais using Facebook: 16,662,060
- Percentage of Thais on Facebook: 24.62%
- Percentage of Thai internet users on Facebook: 93.5%
- Thailand's Facebook usage in global rankings: 16th (just behind Spain and ahead of Japan)
- Company with most Facebook fans in Thailand: Pepsithai
- Media outlet with most Facebook fans in Thailand: KUTE CLUB (a beauty website)
- Gender split of Thai Facebook users: 48% male, 52% female

Five most popular places in Thailand (based on Facebook "likes"):
1. Suvarnabhumi Airport
2. Siam Paragon shopping mall
3. CentralPlaza Ladprao shopping mall
4. Terminal 21 shopping mall
5. Siam Square shopping district

Cities worldwide with the most Facebook users:

City	Number of users
Bangkok	8,682,940
Jakarta	7,434,580
Istanbul	7,066,700
London	6,139,180
Bogota	6,112,120
San Paulo	5,718,220
Mexico City	4,294,820
Santiago	4,129,700
Mumbai	3,700,460

Source: www.socialbakers.com, as of September 2012

THE LAST FIELD MARSHAL
· · · · · · ·

According to Military Ranks Act B.E. 2479, field marshal is the highest rank in the army, navy and air force. The title was created by King Vajiravudh. The last person who received the rank of field marshal was Kriengkrai Attanun, who was bestowed the rank posthumously after a helicopter accident in 1972.

THE KING'S TRIPS ABROAD
· · · · · · ·

Beginning in 1959, His Majesty King Bhumibol Adulyadej made numerous state visits abroad. After his 1967 tour, the king only left Thai soil one more time, for a brief visit to Laos to inaugurate the Friendship Bridge over the Mekong river. The countries that the king has visited since his coronation in 1951:

1959: Vietnam

1960: Indonesia, Burma, United States, United Kingdom, Germany, Portugal, Switzerland, Denmark, Norway, Sweden, Italy, The Vatican State, Belgium, France, Luxembourg, The Netherlands and Spain

1962: Pakistan, Federation of Malaya, New Zealand and Australia

1963: Japan, Republic of China and Philippines

1964: Austria

1966: Germany and Austria

1967: Iran, United States and Canada

1994: Laos

PAD THAI: A MODERN INVENTION
· · · · · · ·

Pad Thai is made by stir-frying rice noodles with eggs, shrimp, bean sprouts, chicken and tofu, and garnishing with local ingredients such as ground roasted peanuts, pickled white radish, scallions, lime and chilli powder. The dish is often served with sliced raw banana flower and Chinese leek. Prime Minister Pibul Songgram and his wife created the recipe for *Pad Thai* during a rice shortage in the 1930s. To reduce the amount of rice consumed, Pibul encouraged people to eat the noodle dish instead. Since then, *Pad Thai* has become one of Thailand's national dishes and is recognised internationally. The best rice noodle to use in *Pad Thai* is called *sen chan*, which means "noodles from Chanthaburi province".

POPULAR FERMENTED FOODS
• • • • • • •

When a foreigner in Thailand tucks into some *sai krok Isaan* or takes his or her *som tam* with *pla ra*, the act can elicit smiles and gasps from Thais impressed by the adventurous choice. Here are some of the more popular fermented favourites and the source.

Local names	Fermented
Pla ra	Freshwater fish
Naem	Pork and pig skin
Kapi	Shrimp
Kao mak	Rice
Sai krok Isaan	Minced pork
Mum	Beef or buffalo meat and liver
Kai yiew ma	Egg

MOST COMMON NICKNAMES
• • • • • • •

Most Thais are given a nickname by their parents when they are born, or acquire one later in life. Used in informal social settings, these nicknames are typically simple words like *mah* (meaning dog), although English words are also common. The most popular nicknames (with English meanings):

Ranking	Females	Males
1	May	Boy
2	Ann	Nueng (one)
3	Kai (chicken)	Ake (first)
4	Noon (fluff)	Chai (male)
5	Tai (rabbit)	Joe
6	Koi (little finger)	Bank
7	Nui (chubby)	Ball
8	Ying (female)	A
9	Fah (blue or sky)	Tui (chubby)
10	Nam (water)	Nick

Source: Ministry of Culture

EVOLUTION OF THE THAI FLAG
· · · · · · ·

Years	Description
Kingdoms of Ayudhya and Thon Buri	Plain red flag
c. 1790–1820 (Rama I era)	Red flag with a white spinning *chakra* disk
c. 1820–1855 (Rama II era)	Same as before but a white elephant was inserted inside the *chakra*
1855–1916	A white elephant against a red backdrop
1917	Red flag with two horizontal white stripes
1917–present	Two red horizontal stripes on the top and bottom, which stand for the nation, followed by two white horizontal stripes symbolising the purity of Buddhism. A blue band in the middle, twice the size of the individual red and white stripes, represents the monarchy. The three colours and their meanings together signify the unofficial motto of the country: "Nation-Religion-King".

DOCUMENTED DOMESTIC VIOLENCE
· · · · · · ·

According to a 2009 survey, women aged 15–19 with no education at all were the most likely to be abused. Other statistics:

- 2.9% of women overall reported abuse
- Women aged 15–19 were the most likely age group to have experienced abuse, at 6.3%
- Women aged 35–39 were second at 3.3% and women aged 40–49 years experience the lowest frequency of abuse at 2.3%
- Only 0.6% of women with a bachelor degree or higher reported abuse

Source: National Statistical Office

FROM "LIM" TO "LIMTHONGKUL"
· · · · · · ·

O ne way to distinguish whether a Thai person has Chinese origins is to look at his or her family name. Thais started to use family names for the first time during the reign of King Vajiravudh. First, names were bestowed by the king himself to the elites and those people associated with the court. Later, commoners were instructed to create a family name too. Typically, the Chinese living in Thailand first used their original one-syllable Chinese last name, which is known as a *sae*. Then, during the era of Field Marshal Pibul Songgram in the 1930s, it became common practice among the Chinese immigrants and their families to adopt a Thai last name in order to further assimilate and protect themselves from the anti-Chinese sentiment of the time. To maintain their Chinese roots they usually kept their *sae* as the first syllable of their Thai family name. Sometimes this name came in the form of the exact Chinese word while other times it was a translation.

Nowadays there are still a small number of Thai-Chinese who use their *sae* solely. However, the majority adopted a longer Thai name beginning with the *sae*. Five common *sae* used in Thailand are Tang, Lim, Lee, Ung and Ngow respectively. The adoption of those *sae* into Thai family names has resulted in the well-known family names of Tangtatsawat, Limthongkul, Leenuttapong, Ungpakorn and Ngowsirimanee.

Sources: www.toptenthailand.com and www.panyathai.or.th

TRADITIONAL PASTIMES
· · · · · · ·

T he bloody fisticuffs and kickboxing of *Muay Thai* and the spectacular team sport of *sepak takraw*, which looks like a mix of volleyball, martial arts and break dancing, are two of the most prominent competitive sports in Thailand. However, Thais also enjoy a range of lesser-known sports and games, among them:

- **Krabi krabong** – This is a traditional martial art dating to the Ayudhya period. The combatants use a combination of swords, staffs and other weapons.
- **Fan dab** – This sport evolved out of *krabi krabong*. The players use one or two rattan swords in a competition similar to fencing.
- **Mak yaek** – A little-known Thai board game focused on strategy and known as *apit sodok* in Malaysia.
- **Mak ruk** – The Thai chess game played by millions around the country originated from the centuries-old Indian ancestors of international chess.
- **Pok deng** – Also called *pok kao*, this card game is an adaptation of baccarat and is popular with gamblers in Thailand.

A PERIOD A LONG TIME AGO
· · · · · · ·

I magine being a woman in Siam 300 years ago and it's that time of the month. A messy situation, yes, we know. Women didn't have sanitary pads (obviously) so they used coconut bract to absorb their blood. First, they had to cut the bract into smaller pieces, before pounding it to make it soft. Then, they would wrap it tightly under a cloth, which they would secure into place by tying it to another cloth around their waist. Some women simply layered many pieces of cloth on top of each other, but that would also mean more laundry and less efficient absorption. The bad news is, if they were so poor that they didn't have extra cloth, they simply had to continue wearing the same stained cloth.

The first disposable sanitary pads were imported during the reign of King Vajiravudh (Rama VI). The brand imported was Kotex and it has become synonymous with sanitary pads in Thailand, in the same way washing detergent is called Fab. For a while, only upperclass women could afford Kotex but eventually pads became more affordable for all.

MOST POPULAR THAI-LANGUAGE GOOGLE SEARCHES IN 2011
· · · · · · ·

Entertainment .... "Kan hu" *
News .... "Flood"
Games .... "Angry Bird"
Communications .... "Facebook"
Gadgets .... "iPhone 5"

* This song's title literally means "itchy ears"; it was used in the talk-of-the-town song and dance video as a sexually suggestive double entendre, referring to a woman's vagina.

Source: Google's 2011 survey

A TASTE FOR TOBACCO
· · · · · · ·

- 47% of men, 3% of women and 24% of the overall population smoke tobacco in Thailand.
- 31% of adults were exposed to tobacco smoke in the workplace.
- 63% of smokers thought about quitting because of the pictorial health warnings featured on cigarette packages.
- 50% of hand-rolled cigarette smokers and smokeless tobacco users thought about quitting because of the black-and-white pictorial health warnings on shredded tobacco packages.

Source: Global Adult Tobacco Survey, World Health Organization

VISITS BY US PRESIDENTS
. . . .

In 1966, Lyndon Baines Johnson became the first sitting American president to visit Thailand. (Ulysses S. Grant visited in 1879, two years after his term had ended.) Richard Nixon visited in 1969, Bill Clinton in 1996, and George W. Bush twice, in 2003 and 2008.

STAY TRUE TO YOUR SCHOOL
. . . .

	School	Motto	Translation
Government schools	Suankularb Wittayalai School	*pu ru di pen pu charoen*	Those who are wise are civilised
	Triam Udom Suksa School	*mi kwam ru ku kunnatham*	Knowledge together with virtue
	Satriwit School	*pueng prapruet tham hai sucharit*	Do every deed with honesty
	Debsirin School	*Mai kuan pen kon rok lok*	One should not be useless to the world
	Rajavinit Matayom School	*sueksa di mi winai fai kitchakum*	Study well, have discipline, be active
Private schools	St. Gabriel College	*manut tuk kon tong tum ngarn kwarm utsaha wiriya pen hontang hang kwam sumret*	Every human being must work; perseverance will lead to success
	St. Joseph Convent School	*sueksa di mi winai jai mettu faiha kunnatham lertlum karnngarn*	Study well, have discipline, have mercy, aim for virtue and excel at work
	Bangkok Christian College	Honesty is the best policy	n/a
	Assumption College	*Wiriya utsaha num ma sueng kwam sumret*	Perseverance leads to success
	Wattana Wittaya Academy	*sutsue mi winai fai sueksa pattana chat terdtun sat kasat*	Maintain honesty, have discipline, strive to be educated, develop the nation, and uphold religion and the monarchy
International schools	Bangkok Patana International School	Fulfilling potential	n/a
	International School Bangkok	Together, we are the best that we can be	n/a
	Ruamrudee International School	To the stars	n/a

BANGKOK VERSUS ISAAN MONTHLY EXPENSES

Average monthly expenditure per household in 2010:

Type of expense	Greater Bangkok (baht per month)	Northeastern (Isaan) region (baht per month)
Food and drinks	8,625	4,726
Alcoholic beverages	349	181
Tobacco products	162	82
Furniture and household equipment	6,421	2,525
Apparel and footwear	591	329
Personal care	849	397
Medical and health care	489	187
Transport and communication	6,048	2,853
Education	840	179
Recreational and religious activities	521	254
Special occasions	75	300
Total	**24,970**	**12,013**

Source: The Household Socio-Economic Survey, National Statistical Office

AVERAGE IQ OF DIFFERENT ASIAN POPULATIONS

IQ tests aim to have a mean score of 100 with 95% of the test takers falling within a standard deviation of 15 points i.e. 95% should score between 85 and 115.

Hong Kong, Singapore	108
North Korea, South Korea	106
Japan, China, Taiwan	105
Vietnam	94
Malaysia	92
Thailand, Cambodia, Brunei	91
Laos	89
Myanmar, Indonesia	87
Philippines	86

Source: Thai PBS

THE KING OF FRUITS
· · · · · · ·

The durian is known as the "King of Fruits" in Southeast Asia because of its distinctive smell, shape, size and taste. Loved by many—and considered revolting by others—the fruit is often banned in hotels, hospitals and public transportation vehicles because of its extremely pungent aroma. Among the nearly 200 types of durian available in Thailand, the most popular are *mon thong* (golden pillow), *cha ni* (gibbon), *kan yao* (long stalk) and *kradum* (buttons). There are also many hybrid varieties with strange names like *kob* (frog) or *katoey* (transvestite). A raw durian can weigh up to seven pounds (3.17 kilogrammes).

Because durian is full of sugar, sulphur and fat, it is generally considered unhealthy for people with diabetes or high blood pressure to consume the fruit. Eating too much durian has even been known to be fatal. Some people believe that durian causes people's body temperature to rise, so it is common for people to eat mangosteens, which are said to help cool the body, along with durian.

FASHION OR FASCISM?
· · · · · · ·

Some people are shocked when they stumble upon a piece of "Nazi chic" in Thailand such as T-shirts bearing cartoonish images of Hitler or WWII-style motorcycle helmets emblazoned with Third Reich insignia. A few incidents (typically based in a lack of understanding about the Holocaust and its sensitivities) have created international headlines:

- 2007 – Students at a Bangkok school held a mock Nazi parade
- 2007 – Thai rock band Slur donned Nazi uniforms for a music video
- 2009 – Louis Tussaud's Waxworks Pattaya erected a large billboard featuring Adolph Hitler in Nazi salute, alongside the slogan (in Thai), "Hitler is not dead"
- 2011 – Choosing Nazi uniforms for their "fancy dress" sports day parade, students at Sacred Heart School in Chiang Mai waved swastika flags and performed Nazi salutes for onlookers
- 2012 – The Israeli ambassador reprimanded a shop owner at Terminal 21 shopping mall for his McHitler doll, which is a cross between Hitler and Ronald McDonald
- 2012 – An angry MP chastised the House Speaker by giving the Nazi salute and shouting, "Heil Hitler, Mr Speaker of the dictatorship, Heil Hitler!"

Sources: CNN, YouTube, Daily Mail, asiancorrespondent.com

THE DAVID BECKHAM TEMPLE
· · · · · · ·

While most temples in Thailand maintain a traditional and timeless ambience and décor, Wat Pariwat in Bangkok pays a small tribute to a contemporary figure, the football legend David Beckham. Inside the temple's chapel, on the far right of the base of the central Buddha shrine, a small relief statue of the English free kick specialist has been added. The statue, which is one foot high and completely covered in gold leaf, shows Beckham with a full head of long hair and wearing his football kit. Although some Thais have objected to it (not many and not very strenuously), the temple's senior monk defended it when interviewed about it more than a decade ago. "Football has become a religion and has millions of followers. So, to be up-to-date, we have to open our minds and share the feelings of millions of people who admire Beckham. This is contemporary art and we want the people of this and the next generation to know what was going on in the year 2000."

Source: BBC, 16 May 2000

OFF TO THE BUFFALO RACES
· · · · · · ·

A furious sprint competition is probably the last thing anyone imagines when they see these rather ungainly looking beasts of burden. But the day before the full moon in the 11th lunar month sees large numbers of tourists, locals and visitors from across the country celebrate the Chon Buri Buffalo Races in Chon Buri province.

For more than 140 years, this competition has been held to celebrate the buffalo's integral role in Thai rice farming and also provide an excuse to eat, drink and be merry.

Up to 300 buffaloes can take part, with between four and six contesting each heat. The owners don't simply pick a tidy example from their normal herds and hope for the best. These buffaloes have been raised and trained specifically to cover the roughly 100-metre course as quickly as possible.

Jockeys enjoy little of the equipment seen in horse racing, or even in North America's famous rodeos. Perched astride the animal's hindquarters, he has only the grip of his legs and a simple bridle formed by stringing a rope through the animal's nose with which to both cling to the beast and direct it.

Like his Western brothers, the Thai buffalo jockey has a crop with which to urge his steed to champion pace. Frequently, this whipping can be a little too successful and the jockey tumbles from his mount (which can weigh 600 kg). There are no helmets or boots to prevent injury. In just T-shirts and shorts, these jockeys truly throw caution to the wind in their bids for lucrative prize money.

CAN'T TOUCH THIS
· · · · · ·

Thai massage is well known around the world. The masseuse uses his or her thumbs, fingers, hands, palms, elbows, arms, knees, and even feet to apply pressure. The massage is performed in four positions—with the customer lying face down, lying face up, lying on the side, and seated. The typical massage commences at the feet and moves upwards to the head.

The following precautions are taken during a Thai massage:

* Do not massage an area with a bone fracture or joint dislocation
* Do not massage someone if they are suffering a fever. The massage will spread the infection if the fever is caused by bacteria. If the fever is caused by muscle inflammation, the massage will also exacerbate the inflammation.
* Do not massage varicose veins
* Do not massage skin infected by a contagious disease
* Do not massage anyone who is under the influence of drugs or alcohol
* Do not apply pressure to lymph nodes
* Special techniques are needed in order to massage a pregnant or menstruating woman
* If the recipient has an overly full stomach, do not have them lie face down and do not give them an abdominal massage

NOT SO THAI: UBIQUITOUS BUT NOT NATIVE
· · · · · ·

Mai Tai cocktail	This fruity cocktail, which uses rum for a base, is believed to have been invented in a bar in California. "Maita'i" is a Tahitian word for "excellent".
Chilli peppers	The chilli pepper is native to South and Central America. It was brought to Europe by European explorers. Thais first experienced the wonderful power of the chilli during the reign of King Narai of the Ayudhya kingdom, when the Portuguese missionaries imported chillies on their ships.
Yen Ta Fo noodles	*Yen ta fo* (fish ball noodle soup with red sauce) originated in China and was invented by the Hakka. This adaptation of common fish ball noodles is made by adding red sauce derived from fermented bean curd.
Water hyacinth	During his visit to Java, King Chulalongkorn discovered the plant and brought it back to be grown in a pond in the palace. Floods spread it to other areas and it has thrived ever since.

HAUNTED PLACES IN BANGKOK AND VICINITY
• • • • • • •

Location	Story
Abandoned Spanish-style house on Soi Ramkamhaeng 32	The house has been abandoned for more than 20 years since a maid was killed there by burglars. After the death, the foreigner who owned the house would hear a woman's plea for help and could not stand living there anymore.
Wat Mahabutr, Phra Kanong	Wat Mahabutr is where the famous legend *Mae Nak Phra Kanong* originated. This ghost story about a woman who died in childbirth while her husband was in the army is still a Thai favourite.
Unused bus depot on Soi Saiyood	In the past, wrecked buses were brought here after accidents. People reported seeing the wrecked buses' headlights turn on, and some taxi drivers said a man in front of the garage would disappear once they stopped to pick him up.
Traditional Thai-style house on Soi Rod-Anan 1 on Sukhapiban 1 Road	The owner of the house was an old lady and people believe her spirit dwells there. Some children see her scolding them when they play in front of the house. Those who dared enter it heard an old lady's voice shouting to chase them out.
Torched house on Rangsit Klong 13	A woman burned to death in the house and neighbours say they sometimes hear her scream.
Abandoned factory on Soi Kasem Bundit University, Pattanakan Road	This abandoned pen factory is believed to host an angry guardian spirit on its premises. When it was operational, there were several accidental deaths. Some people believe that knocking the water tank three times will make the guardian spirit appear.
Wat Prasart, Nonthaburi	In the back of this ancient temple built in the Ayudhya period are the ruins of the home of noblewoman *Phra nang* Usawadee Devee. It is believed that anyone who enters this area and acts with disrespect will invite misfortune.
Abandoned factory on Soi 2, Bangpu Industrial Estate	An explosion at this shoe factory killed many workers. After that, many remaining workers left and the business collapsed. The owner shot himself in the office on the top floor of the factory.
Unfinished European-style house on Soi Watcharapol	While under construction, the owner and his family were all killed in a car accident. People sometimes see a man, a woman and a child in the house.
Abandoned village on Soi Watcharapol	Piyaporn Village was constructed on land that used to be a graveyard without the proper ceremony to inform the guardian spirits. During construction there were many accidents, including the death of two children in the manmade lake inside the village.

Source: www.toptenthailand.com

WHEN PATTAYA FIRST MADE ITS NAME
· · · · · · ·

This verbatim excerpt about a new seaside resort from the *Bangkok Post* column "The Postmen Say" was printed on 3 May 1958:

"That a new vacation spot has risen in Pataya Beach, Cholburi, and you should go there one weekend during this hot season, if you have a car or can beg, borrow or steal one, and some money. (Car thieves have to be extra careful. A police radio car is stationed on Sukhumvit Highway, at a road block, 24 hours a day).

You drive along the highway, past Cholburi town, past Bangsaen, past Sriraja, past Banglamoong. At the 141st kilometer you come to a small market. Turn right, drive down a gravel-and-sand path for about four kilometers and you come to Pataya Beach.

If you reach there at high tide, you will see a magnificent bay. A cape of rocks juts out at your right, a long low line of undulating hills on your left. In between you find clear, almost smooth, blue water.

There is nothing like it at Bangsaen or even Hua Hin.

On this sheltered bay, you can drive a speedboat or you can ski. And speedboat-driving and water-skiing and swimming were what the fun-lovers, the young, the old, the middle-aged, the vacationers, the escapists, the idle rich, the extravagant middle class, the low wage-earners who shared but expenses, were doing last Sunday when some of us made a trip there.

There was no surf-riding because there was no surf.

The sand is golden and clean. Along the beach have sprung up smart bungalows, some belonging to private persons who have made their fortunes in politics or business, and some built for renting-out.

Some of the vacationers had come with makeshift tents which were pitched on the sand.

There was a holiday atmosphere in the air ...

The beach is just right. The sea is excellent for swimming. Motor-boating, skiing, fishing. The scenery is uplifting. The crowd is not so large as to cause discomfort.

The only trouble is that when you drive there you may feel it is a little too far, especially as the road in some sections is not too smooth, though the whole way is asphalted, up to and beyond the side-path leading to the beach ..."

CREATING THE CONSTITUTION
· · · · · · ·

Since 1932, when Thailand became a constitutional monarchy, there have been 18 constitutions (three interim ones and 15 "permanent" ones).

Once a new constitution is approved, officials will write it by hand onto a traditional white booklet gilded with gold leaf, and His Majesty the King will sign it. Three of these original editions are created. One is kept at the Parliament, one at Government House, and another at the Grand Palace.

Source: www.whereisthailand.info

FIELD MASHAL P. WEIRD
· · · · · · ·

He is one of the most famous figures in Thai history, so you would assume everyone could agree on his name and how to spell it in English. Problem is Pibul Songgram, also known as Phibunsongkhram (and other variations), born Plaek Khitasangkha, was called several names over the decades (not always nice ones). The dynamic prime minister and military dictator who dramatically influenced Thailand with his cultural mandates in the 1930s and 1940s was named "Plaek" ("weird" or "strange") by his parents when he was born, owing to what they saw as his unusual appearance—his ears were noticeably lower than his eyes. When he rose through the military ranks, he was given the title Luang Phibunsongkhram by King Prajadhipok and then, as was common, adopted the title as his own surname. But Westerners simply referred to him as Phibun (also spelled Pibul or Phibul depending on the source), and thus his name has frequently been written as if Phibun was his first name and Songkhram his last (e.g. Phibun Songkhram). Clear as mud? No wonder that as field marshal (the highest military rank), the man born "Plaek" preferred to be called simply Field Marshal P. At that time, using only an initial for one's name was trendy, leading to yet another variation on his name.

Sources: *Bangkok Post*, *A History of Thailand* by Chris Baker and Pasuk Phongpaichit

THE THAI RIDGEBACK
· · · · · · ·

The Thai Ridgeback, named after the ridge of hair that runs along its back, is the most common breed of dog found in Thailand. According to the Thai Ridgeback Dog Club, the breed has many charming traits and distinguishing characteristics:

- Clean
- Good temper and spirit
- Intelligent and alert
- Independent
- Self-reliant, cautious and vigilant
- Not destructive of its surroundings
- Quiet and calm
- Strong fighting skills
- Great memory and recall
- Possessive of its master
- Adaptable

INCOME OF THE CROWN PROPERTY BUREAU
· · · · · · ·

The Crown Property Bureau (CPB) is the financial arm of the Thai monarchy, and is entrusted with managing its land holdings and wealth. The income of the CPB is derived from three primary sources: Siam Commercial Bank, Siam Cement Group, and its properties.

As of 2011, the CPB:

- Had a 23% stake in Siam Commercial Bank, which delivered the CPB an income of 2.5 billion baht in 2010.
- Had a 32% stake in Siam Cement Group, which delivered CPB an income of 3.4 billion baht in 2010.
- Owned a total of 41,000 *rai* of land, with 8,300 *rai* in Bangkok, mostly in the historic centre. The CPB's income from its properties was 2.5 billion baht in 2010.

Therefore, the total income from these three sources in 2010 was approximately US$271,000,000.

Source: *King Bhumibol Adulyadej: A Life's Work;* note: 1 *rai* equals 1,600 square metres.

DELAYED: SUVARNABHUMI INTERNATIONAL AIRPORT TIMELINE
· · · · · · ·

1961 – The Ministry of Transport conducts a survey designating an area in Samut Prakan province as suitable for Bangkok's new international airport.

1973 – A total of 8,000 acres of land in Samut Prakan province is acquired by the government. The project is shelved after the October 1973 student uprising.

1978 – A company commissioned by the Ministry of Transport confirms that the land is still suitable, but the project stalls.

1991 – The Cabinet under Prime Minister Anand Panyarachun greenlights construction of a new international airport with the Airports Authority of Thailand (AAT) as the responsible agency.

1995 – The area known as "Cobra Swamp" in Samut Prakan province is chosen as the site of the new airport.

2000 – His Majesty the King names the airport Suvarnabhumi, which means "Golden Land".

2001–2006 – The government led by Thaksin Shinawatra aggressively pushes the airport's construction, which eventually becomes mired in corruption allegations.

2006 – Ten days after the coup that ousted Thaksin Shinawatra from power, the airport officially opens.

THE WORRY REPORT
· · · · · · ·

The United Nations Development Programme (UNDP) released its "Thailand National Human Development Report" in 2009. One of the topics is human security. The following table lists the concerns and worries of Thai people—from a survey sample that included local officials from departments and agencies engaged in social issues, and representatives of local civil society, including village headmen, elected members of local government, social development volunteers, health volunteers, religious leaders, as well as representatives of the aged, disabled and other groups.

Personal concerns

High concern
- Being involved in a traffic accident
- Being sick from bad food
- Becoming sick from pesticides
- Becoming seriously ill
- Suffering from drought
- Not having enough money in old age
- Not being able to get good quality health care
- Children or friends becoming addicted to drugs

Medium concern
- Being robbed
- Being a victim of an insurgency attack
- Not having help in old age
- Suffering loss of income
- Suffering from floods
- Not being able to afford the high cost of health care
- Being asked for a bribe from police

Low concern
- Being subjected to violence at home
- Becoming unemployed
- Being asked for a bribe from officials
- Losing savings in a bank collapse
- Forced to move for economic reasons

Social concerns

High concern
- Corruption among politicians
- Human trafficking
- Decline of the environment
- More immigrants coming to Thailand
- Deforestation
- Corruption among officials
- Political disorder
- Poor quality of education
- High cost of fuel

Medium concern
- Foreigners buying land
- Contaminated food
- Growing indebtedness
- Conflicts over the environment
- Air pollution
- Government not responsive to the people
- Contaminated water
- Thailand not competitive in the world

Low concern
- Wide gap between rich and poor
- Ageing society
- Hazardous waste
- Wide gap between city and village
- High cost of rice
- Contracting bird flu
- Noise pollution
- Victimisation by the police

THAI FILMS HONOURED ABROAD
· · · · · · ·

Year	Title and director	Awards
1954	*Santi-Veena* by Rattana Pestonji	Best cinematography and best art director at the Asia-Pacific Film Festival Best Asian cultural presentation from the Golden Harvest Awards
1985	*The Butterfly and the Flowers* by Yuthana Mookdasanit	Best film at the East-West Film Festival
2002	*Blissfully Yours* by Aphichatpong Weerasethakul	Prix Un Certain Regard at the Cannes Film Festival
2004	*Tropical Malady* by Aphichatpong Weerasethakul	Jury Prize at the Cannes Film Festival
2010	*Uncle Boonmee Who Can Recall His Past Lives* by Aphichatpong Weerasethakul	Palme d'Or at the Cannes Film Festival Best film from Asian Film Award

Aphichatpong Weerasethakul

WHAT THEY ARE EATING IN FIRST CLASS
· · · · · · ·

Royal First Class, the premium seating provided by Thailand's national airline, THAI, also includes exclusive fast-track immigration channels and a lounge equipped with a wide range of facilities, even a spa and sauna. Once on board, your meal will be served at any time as requested and foods can be pre-ordered. Almost 40 dishes are available. These include:

- Lobster Thermidor
- Grilled fillet of beef Rossini
- Lamb Saltimbocca
- Scallop Provençale
- Glass noodles *Pad Thai*
- Fish/prawn *chu-chee*
- Assorted sushi
- Chilean sea bass with X.O. sauce
- Chinese roast duck with noodles
- Rice with steamed chicken (*kao man kai*)
- Fish maw with crab meat soup

The price of a first-class return ticket from Bangkok to London starts at 193,605 baht (US$6,250), as of September 2012.

Source: www.thaiairways.com

MARRIAGE BY THE NUMBERS
· · · · · · ·

Of the 12.8 million women aged 15–49 years who were married by 2009:
- 73% were married to a man older than themselves
- 33% had husbands who were five or more years older than themselves
- 11% were the same age as their husbands
- 15% were older than their husbands
- The average age difference between spouses was 4.4 years

Source: National Statistic Office Thailand

WATERY WISDOM
· · · · · · ·

M any proverbs and sayings in Thai focus around water—not surprising given that Thais have been plagued by drought and floods for centuries, grow rice in water, fish the many rivers, and Bangkok's infrastructure was previously focused on its canals.

Proverb	Literal Meaning	What It Really Means
Pan nam pen tua	Mould water into a shape (i.e. ice; Thais were originally shocked that one could make ice)	Used to describe someone who lies frequently and makes bizarre excuses
Nam kuen hai rib tak	When the tide rises, hurry to get some water	When the opportunity presents itself, seize it
Son chorakae hai wai nam	Teaching a crocodile how to swim	Used when teaching or talking about a subject that someone already knows well
Nam ning lai luek	Still water runs deep	Used to describe someone who may be quiet and polite, but is actually quite intellectual and astute
Nam ma pla kin mot, nam lot mot kin pla	When the tide rises, the fish eats the ant, when the tide goes down the ant eats the fish	What goes around comes around
Nam noi yom pae fai	A small amount of water will not put out a fire	If you are not adequately prepared or qualified, you are not likely to triumph
Ya wang nam bo na	Don't depend on the next pond of water	Don't wait for the next opportunity or leave important issues until later
Nam tuam pak	A mouth flooded with water	Used when a person is unable to say something due to fear
Kin nam tai sok	Drinking water off of another's elbow	Usually to describe how "minor wives" must be satisfied living with leftovers and receiving second-best treatment compared to the first wife
Nam lot to put	When the water recedes the stump appears	Used to explain the wrongdoing of people in power. Once they lose power, all the wrongdoing will be exposed.

WHEN THE STUDENTS CHANGED HISTORY ...
· · · · · · ·

The following is the text of the leaflet distributed by students who initiated the Anti-Japanese Goods Week in late 1972. The boycott was one of a series of events that empowered student groups (especially The National Students Center) and gave them a political voice, ultimately leading to the successful overthrow of the military-run government in 1973.

Dear Thai citizens,

We, the students, who are also your children are co-operating with one another to refrain from buying Japanese goods during the Anti-Japanese Goods Week.

The reason is that Japan is taking advantage of us by using various business ploys to cheat us and also because the trade dominance of the Japanese in Thailand has increased alarmingly during the past 10 years putting Thailand gradually into a position as "Japan's economic slave".

This feeling is not far from reality if you study carefully the action of Japan or look around and see Japanese dominance in the trade and cultural spheres.

We would not have been in trouble at all if the Japanese role was to help develop our country's economy as they often used to imply.

However we will not bear injustices in business practices which only seek one-sided benefit or force, squeeze and underprice Thai commodities without thinking of the damage, injustice or the troubles caused to the Thai people.

We are also not pleased with the Japanese who take job opportunities from us by violating the law and also with government officials' apathy for the situation.

If we have a look at numerous Japanese goods which have glutted Thai markets and become a part of the everyday life of Thais influenced by advertising (made by Japanese firms), a large number of them are not essential at all. Furthermore, they will cause more damage to the national economy.

The co-operation to refrain from buying Japanese goods is a means to solve this problem.

It also shows that the Thai are ready to join their efforts to protect the national interests, no matter what the issue may be.

We do not want violence because we realize the need for international relations. But if robbers come to our house we have to seriously fight them until they flee or stop being what they are.

This movement may be only an insignificant starting point but it needs co-operation from every sector as it is the fight for righteousness and national progress.

The National Students Center therefore asks you to sacrifice your happiness and conveniences, and to save the money you may spend from buying and using Japanese goods and services during the Anti-Japanese Goods Week November 20–30, to show that the Thai blood runs thick and cannot be looked down on by anyone.

–The National Students Center, 16 November 1972

ONE MANLY MAN TOO MANY
· · · · · · ·

When various herbs are mixed with rice whiskey and then allowed to infuse for a few weeks, you get *yaa dong lao* ("alcohol-pickled medicine") or *yaa dong* for short, a popular, traditional medicinal drink served by street vendors to boost energy or remedy everything from fatigue to indigestion to a flagging libido. Contained in large vats, these home brews are made from hundreds of different recipes and possible ingredients. Some examples of the names given to *yaa dong* concoctions:

* Towering Dragon
* Tiger Force
* Male Elephant Power
* Rama Goes to War
* Tribesman Carrying Buffalo
* Horse Bursts His Stable

* Manly Man
* Moaning Mistress
* Never Flaccid
* Murmuring Lady
* Old Man Rapes Elephant

Source: *Very Thai: Everyday Popular Culture* by Philip Cornwel-Smith

ISANOSAURUS ATTAVIPATCHI
· · · · · · ·

Thailand is proud to lay claim to its own species of dinosaur, known as the Isanosaurus. Its fossils, discovered in the Isaan (northeastern) region, suggest that it is one of the first sauropod dinosaurs (meaning all four feet were on the ground). It is believed to have lived during the Late Triassic period 210 million years ago.

Indeed, dinosaur fossils have been found all over the Isaan region, in provinces such as Loei, Mukdahan, Khon Kaen and Chaiyaphum. The first dinosaur fossil was found in 1976 and, over the last three decades, around 10,000 more have been discovered nationwide.

Kalasin province is believed to have the highest concentration. The Sirindhorn Museum and Phu Kum Khao Dinosaur Excavation Site in Kalasin contain the largest collection of fossils and are popular tourist attractions. More than 200,000 people visit the museum each year, mostly schoolchildren.

Sources: *The New York Times*, *The Dinosauria*

GOOGLE: BLOCKED BY OFFICIAL REQUEST
• • • • • • •

Government agencies and courts around the world regularly ask Google to remove content from its services. Content may be removed for various reasons such as breaches of local laws and alleged defamation. In some cases, content is removed completely. In others, Google blocks access from certain parts of the world. Everything Google removed in the reporting periods below was on the YouTube video-streaming service.

July–December 2011

- Government requests to remove content: 4
- Number of items removed: 149
- Google's explanation: "We received four requests from the Ministry of Information, Communication and Technology to remove 149 YouTube videos for allegedly insulting the monarchy in violation of Thailand's *lèse-majesté* law. We restricted 70% of these videos from view in Thailand in accordance with local law."

January–June 2011

- Government requests to remove content: 2
- Number of items removed: 225
- Google's explanation: "We received two requests from the Ministry of Information, Communication and Technology in Thailand to remove 225 YouTube videos for allegedly insulting the monarchy in violation of Thailand's *lèse-majesté* law. We restricted Thai users from accessing more than 90% of the videos."

July–December 2010

- Government requests to remove content: 1
- Number of items removed: 43
- Google's explanation: "We received a request from the Ministry of Information, Communication and Technology in Thailand to remove 43 pieces of content because they were mocking or criticizing the king in violation of Thai *lèse-majesté* laws. We restricted Thai users from accessing these videos."

January–June 2010

- Government requests to remove content: 0
- Number of items removed: 0

By comparison, from July 2011 to December 2011, the US government made 187 requests leading to the removal of 6,192 items. China simply blocks all access to YouTube and limits access to other Google services.

Source: Google Transparency Report

POPULAR MEDITATION POSTURES
• • • • • • •

Widely practised by devout Buddhists in Thailand, meditation helps improve one's level of concentration and also helps to bring peace of mind. There are three popular positions for practising mediation in Thailand:

1. Walking meditation – Concentrate on each step, and focus on the feeling of "raising", "lifting", "pushing" and "dropping" the sole of the foot.

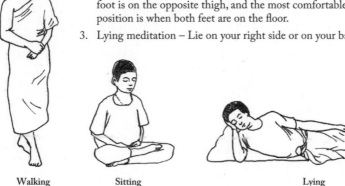

2. Sitting meditation – Sitting meditation can be performed in three poses, depending on the skill of each practitioner. Full lotus is when the soles of both feet are uppermost on the opposite thigh. Half lotus is when only one foot is on the opposite thigh, and the most comfortable and the easiest position is when both feet are on the floor.

3. Lying meditation – Lie on your right side or on your back.

Walking   Sitting   Lying

TAKING P.C. TO NEW HEIGHTS
• • • • • • •

Hiring men to work as cabin attendants is nothing new, but you may be surprised to learn that a new Thai airline recruits them to work as *female* crew. In 2010 P.C. Air became the first carrier in the world to specifically recruit transsexuals for its cabin crew.

P.C. Air's tag line is "I believe it's 'my way'", a reference to the company's stated aim of taking the famous warmth, hospitality and tolerance of Thailand to new heights by providing a premium service in an atmosphere dedicated to equality.

The airline, which says it prides itself on "Service Beyond Expectation", is the brainchild of Thai Peter Chan. In October 2011, P.C. Air received its first plane, an Airbus A310-200 leased from Singapore's Phoenix Aircraft Leasing, and the carrier's maiden flight, a demonstration for members of the media, took place on 15 December 2011.

Sources: P.C. Air, *Bangkok Post*, flightglobal.com

ARE WE THERE YET?
• • • • • • •

Distances to different major global cities:

New York, US	13,923 km	(8651 miles)
Los Angeles, US	13,293 km	(8260 miles)
Vancouver, Canada	11,799 km	(7331 miles)
Madrid, Spain	10,175 km	(6323 miles)
London, UK	9526 km	(5919 miles)
Paris, France	9439 km	(5865 miles)
Rome, Italy	8825 km	(5483 miles)
Berlin, Germany	8599 km	(5343 miles)
Stockholm, Sweden	8264 km	(5135 miles)
Sydney, Australia	7531 km	(4680 miles)
Moscow, Russia	7061 km	(4388 miles)
Dubai, UAE	4883 km	(3034 miles)
Tokyo, Japan	4604 km	(2861 miles)
Beijing, China	3692 km	(2294 miles)
New Delhi, India	2916 km	(1812 miles)
Hong Kong	1724 km	(1071 miles)

Source: Tourism Authority of Thailand

SUDDEN UNEXPLAINED DEATH SYNDROME
• • • • • • •

Sudden Unexplained Death Syndrome (SUDS), called *lai tai* in Thailand, kills otherwise healthy men aged 20–49, often while they sleep. Almost exclusively, it victimises men from Southeast Asia, primarily from Thailand's northeast, and also from the Hmong tribe, who inhabit Laos, China and Vietnam in addition to Thailand. Many suspected cases of SUDS have been ascribed to the consumption of sticky rice and large volumes of alcohol. However, autopsies have found no underlying causes to explain the deaths. Apart from genetic connections, researchers have linked SUDS to an abnormal heartbeat condition known as Brugada Syndrome. Some Thais blame the deaths on the vengeful "widow ghost" named *phi mae mai,* who is said to claim a young man's life at night. Similarly, in Laos, the problem is known as *dab tsog,* the night phantom. During one period of frequent media reports about Thai labourers dying overseas from SUDS, men from the northeast region slept dressed as women in order to trick the "widow ghost".

Sources: *British Medical Journal, Journal of the Medical Association of Thailand, The Cambridge World History of Human Disease*

'DERNN SLANG DERIVED FROM ENGLISH
• • • • • • •

Don't be *'noid* when you use the following Thai slang derived from English words to sound *cree-ate*.

Slang	Derived From	Meaning	How To Use It
Freshy	Freshman	A first-year student in university	"That *freshy* girl could really use a nose job."
Cree-ate	Creative	Used to compliment creative things or people	"Omigosh, the presentation of the food on my plate is sooo *cree-ate!*"
'Noid	Paranoid	Someone who is obsessively worried about something	"What are you smoking? You are so *'noid* today."
'Tist	Artist	Someone who is "indie", behaves differently, thinks too much and slips into a personal world a lot	"She's so *'tist* sometimes; I think she needs a backhand slap to bring her back to reality."
'Dernn	Modern	Used to describe something trendy or cool	"Look at my iPhone5! Even my mom says it's so *'dernn!*"
Fin	Finish/finale	Originally relating to an orgasm but now referring to anything outstanding or euphoric	"That *Batman* movie was sooo *fin!*"
'Verrr	Overreact/over the top	Used to describe melodramatic people or excessive behaviour	"Don't slam the door on me. That's so *'verrr.*"

A BRIEF HISTORY OF RED BULL
• • • • • • •

- *Krating Daeng*, which means "red bull" in Thai, is the name of the popular energy drink created by Chaleo Yoovidhaya in 1975.

- In 1984, Chaleo partnered with an Austrian businessman, Dietrich Matschitz, to launch the energy drink in Austria under the brand name "Red Bull".

- Internationally, Red Bull uses slightly different ingredients than the product sold in Thailand. Red Bull in Thailand is not carbonated.

- The amount of caffeine in a 250 ml can of the international Red Bull is 80 mg, which is less caffeine than is found in an average 250 ml cup of coffee. However, Thai law stipulates that caffeine in energy drinks cannot exceed 50 ml per container.

- Red Bull is banned in some countries, such as Uruguay and Iceland, due to the quantity of caffeine and taurine.

- Before his death in March 2012, Chaleo Yoovidhya was ranked by *Forbes* as the world's 205th richest man, with assets worth more than US$5 billion.

Sources: www.redbull.com, www.forbes.com

THE COMPOSITIONS OF THE KING
• • • • • • •

His Majesty King Bhumibol Adulyadej has been an avid jazz fan since his youth and plays several instruments. As monarch, he has been known to gather his band at night and jam until the wee hours. The king has composed 48 pieces of music that range from jazz songs to marches, ballet suites to blues numbers. A list of his original compositions:

1946
- *Saeng Tien* (Candlelight Blues)
- *Yam Yen* (Love At Sundown)
- *Sai Fon* (Falling Rain)
- *Klai Rung* (Near Dawn)

1947
- *Chata Cheewit* (The H.M. Blues)
- *Duangjai Kab Kwam Rak* (Never Mind the Hungry Men's Blues)

1948
- *March Rajavallop* (Royal Guards March)

1949
- *Arthit Upsaeng* (Blue Day)
- *Theva Pa Kufan* (Dream of Love, Dream of You)
- *Kam Wan* (Sweet Words)
- *Maha Chulalongkorn* (Chulalongkorn University Alma Mater song)
- *Kaewta Kwanjai* (Love Light In My Heart)

1952
- *Porn Pee Mai* (New Year Greetings)
- *Rak Kuen Ruen* (Love Over Again)
- *Yam Kam* (Twilight)
- *Yim Su* (Smiles)
- *March Thongchai Chalermphol* (The Colors March)

1954
- *Mue Som Song* (I Never Dream)
- *Lom Naow* (Love In Spring)
- *Suk Sanyalak* (Friday Night Rag)

1955
- *Oh I Say*
- *Can't You Ever See*
- *Lay Kram Goes Dixie*
- *Kham Laeo* (Lullaby)

1957
- *Sai Lom* (I Think Of You)
- *Klaikangwol* (When)

1958
- *Sang Duen* (Magic Beam)

1959
- *Fan* (Somewhere Somehow)
- *March Rajananawikayothin* (Royal Marines March)
- *Pirom Rak* (The Kinari Suite: A Love Story)
- *Nature Waltz*
- *The Hunter*
- *Kinari Waltz*
- *Pandin Kong Rao* (Alexandra)
- *Phra Mahamongkol*

1963
- *Yung Thong* (Thammasat University Alma Mater song)

1965
- *Duangjai Niran* (Still On My Mind)
- *Tuen Jai* (Old-Fashioned Melody)
- *Rai Duen* (No Moon)
- *Koh Nai Fan* (Dream Island)
- *Waew* (Echo)

1966
- Kasetsart University Alma Mater song

1971
- *Kwam Fan An Soong Sud*

1976
- *Rao Su*
- *Rao Lao Rab 21*

1979
- *Blues for Uthit*

1995
- *Rak* (Love)
- *Menu Kai*

Source: *Bangkok Post*, 10 January 2006

"NOTTHENATION": THE WEBSITE YOU CAN TRUST
• • • • • • •

Www.notthenation.com is an anonymously run website offering satirical news stories about Thailand and the world in the style of The Onion website. NotTheNation, which went live in December 2007, was originally a close copy of *The Nation* newspaper's website before being redesigned several years later. A selection of headlines from the website's archives:

- Bumrungrad Hospital Officially Declared Islam's Third Holiest Site
- Thailand, Cambodia Sign 10-Year Nationalist Fervor Incitement Pact
- Health Ministry Warns Of Mormon Outbreak
- World Media Insists All Of Thailand On Fire, All Thais Dead
- Hundreds Gathering At Last Quiet Spot In Bangkok
- Expat Woman Who Pays Too Much For Everything Says Bangkok Expensive
- World Pizza Council Revokes Pizza Company's Use Of Word "Pizza"
- Bar Staff, Sex Tourists Wait Patiently For White Woman To Get Off Go-Go Stage
- Sukhumbhand Proposes Building New "SkyBangkok" On Top Of Old One
- Pheu Thai Nominates Thaksin's Sister For PM In Stunning Display Of Meritocracy, Progressive Thinking
- Steven Seagal's Career Found Dead In Bangkok

Source: www.notthenation.com

REPRODUCTIVE HEALTH INDICATORS
• • • • • • •

- 15% of married men or women aged 15–49 years received pre-marital contraceptive counselling from health personnel
- 22% of married men or women aged 15–49 years received pre-marital screening for thalassemia or HIV
- 23: Mean age at which women aged 15–49 years gave birth for the first time
- 15% of women exclusively breastfed a child under 6 months
- 36% of women aged 15–59 years had a correct understanding of AIDS and how it is transmitted
- 3% of married women aged 15–49 years experienced spousal abuse in the past year
- 85% of adolescents aged 15–24 years received formal instruction in sex education, family planning and reproductive tract infections

Source: National Statistical Office (Thailand-wide survey).

SHOWING ITS TRUE COLOURS
• • • • • • •

Thais aren't shy about sticking a ridiculous or distasteful sticker on their car bumper. One of the strangest announces that the colour of the car is different from the actual colour. Example: a white car might have a sticker that states, "This car is black". Why would anyone make such a seemingly ridiculous statement? The reason is superstition. If the colour of the car someone is driving is considered unlucky for them, the owner can solve this problem by fixing a sticker on it that states that the colour of their car is actually something else. Apparently, this trick will help ward off any bad luck that your car would otherwise bring to you.

FIELD MARSHAL SARIT AND HIS ASSETS
• • • • • • •

Field Marshal Sarit Thanarat, one of Thailand's most famous leaders, died of cirrhosis of the liver on 8 December 1963. Sarit was rather notorious for his unhealthy lifestyle and merciless approach to enemies and criminal elements, but he was also widely admired for bringing stability and economic development to Thailand after years of coups and counter-coups. Details publicised after his death, however, spoiled his legacy and led to one of the biggest scandals in Thai history. Claims made over his estate revealed not only the vast extent of his ill-gotten wealth (Sarit was on the board of 22 companies), but also the many women the married prime minister had become entangled with—newspapers reported that more than 50 women ("minor wives") and their children had come forward to grab a piece of the pie. An investigation revealed that Sarit had 2.8 billion baht in assets (US$140 million) including:

- 51 automobiles
- More than 22,000 *rai* of land
- A brewery and trust company
- US$12 million funnelled from the national lottery to pseudononymous bank accounts

Overall, US$17.8 million of his estate was traced back to the government sources. US$600,000 had been distributed by Sarit to his minor wives before he died. To settle the claims over his inheritance, the Cabinet decided that the government could seize Sarit's estate. US$32 million was reportedly transferred back to the state.

Sources: *Chronicle of Thailand: Headline News Since 1946*, *A History of Thailand* by Chris Baker and Pasuk Phongpaichit

135

THE RULES OF TINGLISH
• • • • • • •

Common mispronunciations of English words and improper usage are often due to nuances of the Thai language. For example, some sounds in English simply do not exist in Thai. Sometimes Thais pronounce the silent letters in English words. Some struggle to make the sound of consecutive consonants and thus add an extra syllable to the word to compensate. Some omit or use incorrect articles, declensions and conjugations. Frequently they omit the pronoun (allowed in Thai) or the verb "to be". Of course, these types of mistakes are common among anyone trying to speak a foreign language.

Some examples of Tinglish nuances:

- "album" becomes *alabum* or "snore" becomes *sahnore*
- "central" becomes *centran* as Thais often pronounce an "l" as an "n" sound
- "card" becomes *gart* as the "c" is made into a soft "g" sound and "d" is pronounced "t"
- Owing to direct translation from their own speech, Thais may say: *Can you please open the light?* or *I play computer* instead of "I am using the computer"
- "I don't have money" becomes *I no have money*
- *I love you too much* means "I love you very much".
- *Go far far!* is a direct Thai translation of "Get lost!"

HOUSE OF HORRORS OR MUSEUM?
• • • • • • •

Inside Siriraj Hospital, there are 13 exhibition spaces where the public can learn about medicine. One of the most popular museums is the Forensic Museum, which presents interesting and sickening artefacts and exhibits related to forensics medicine in Thailand.

Among the museum's exhibits are:

- The preserved body of See Ooi, Thailand's most famous serial killer. It is preserved in formaldehyde and displayed in a glass box.
- Some skulls that were used to recreate the gunshot wound of King Ananda, who died of a single bullet to the head in 1946; there are also forensic tools used in the case on display.
- Clothes and evidence from the Nuanchawee trial, a scandalous murder case from the 1960s in which a well-to-do doctor killed his fiancée.
- Dead bodies which have undergone almost no decomposition.
- Preserved organs damaged by poisons and cancer.
- Foetuses in different stages of development, including rare cases such as Siamese twins and defective development.
- Weapons from suicide and murder cases.

IMPORTED TELEVISION SHOWS
• • • • • • •

Title	Start	Type of show	Originated from	Status
Games Seth Thee	2000	Game show	Britain's *Who Wants To Be a Millionaire?*	Last show aired in 2008
Weakest Link: Kamchad chud on	2002	Game show	Britain's *The Weakest Link*	Cancelled after Season 2 ended in 2003
Academy Fantasia	2004	Reality show with singing contest	Mexico's *La Academia*	Nine seasons as of 2012
Big Brother	2005	Reality show	Netherlands' *Big Brother* series	Cancelled after Season 2 ended in 2006
Thailand's Got Talent	2011	Talent show	*Britain's Got Talent* series	Season 2 aired in 2012
The Voice	2012	Reality talent show	America's *The Voice*	Season 1 began in 2012

LIFE UNDERGROUND
• • • • • • •

Bangkok's underground train system is managed by the Mass Rapid Transit Authority of Thailand (MRTA). The underground currently has only one line (officially known as the "Chaloem Ratchamongkhon Line") and 18 stations. The lowest fare is 15 baht and the highest is 40 baht.

Some other MRTA facts:
• 651 people are employed by the MRTA
• 190,941 passengers (as of September 2011) use the underground daily
• the underground line generates 4,551,981 baht (about US$147,000) per day in revenue

According to the authority's annual report, the list of "untoward" incidents that occurred in the fiscal year 2011 (October 2010 to September 2011) were:
• 10 accidents
• 12 cases of theft
• 1 case of passenger sickness
• 1 brawl
• 3 incidents of sexual "obscenity"
• 4 cases of passenger offence in relation to MRTA Act B.E. 2543 (such as not paying the fare, damaging property, posting notices)
• 5 cases of detection of a suspicious object

Source: MRTA

WHERE THE WILD THINGS ARE
· · · · · · ·

Some fascinating creatures that call Thailand home:

Water monitor: Tourists often freak out at the sight of these large lizards, which can be spotted around ponds in the parks in the heart of Bangkok. After the Komodo dragon, the water monitor is the world's second-biggest lizard. Typically up to 2 metres long and weighing 10 to 20 kilogrammes, they can sometimes reach a length of 3 metres and a weight of 90 kilogrammes. The Thai word for this animal (*hia*) is a powerful profanity.

Mekong giant catfish: The Mekong giant catfish can be as long as 3.2 metres and weigh as much as 300 kilogrammes. Conservationists are battling to save it from extinction.

Giant freshwater stingray: The giant freshwater stingray is found in northern Australia, as well as Southeast Asia, including Bangkok's Chao Phraya River. They grow to more than 300 kilogrammes and 3 to 4 metres across, with anecdotal reports offering weights exceeding 600 kilogrammes, and yes, the sting is deadly.

Wild water buffalo: The larger wild cousin of the domesticated water buffalo can weigh more than 1,200 kilogrammes. This endangered species has been wiped out in neighbouring Laos and Cambodia, but some wild water buffalo still inhabit Thailand.

Gaur: Weighing up to 1,500 kilogrammes, the gaur is the largest of all wild cattle. Today, this native of South and Southeast Asia is considered vulnerable to extinction and fewer than 1,000 are thought to remain in Thailand.

Asian two-horned rhinoceros: Standing no taller than 1.4 meters at the shoulder, the Asian two-horned rhinoceros is the smallest of the rhinos. It can still weigh up to a tonne, though. Its natural habitat once stretched from India to Borneo, but today it is found in Thailand only in wilderness reserves. Elsewhere, it faces extinction.

CHARGED WITH LÈSE MAJESTÉ
· · · · · · ·

A rticle 112 of the penal code states: "Whoever defames, insults or threatens the king, the queen, the heir apparent, or the regent, shall be punished with imprisonment of three to fifteen years". Anyone can make a complaint that this law has been broken and then the police must decide whether or not to file charges.

From 1956 to 1976, there were an average of 5 charges per year. After the political crisis of 1976, there was an average of 10 charges per year between 1977 and 1992. From 1993 to 2004, the numbers dropped by half and there were no charges brought in 2002. However, the number of *lèse-majesté* charges has spiked dramatically in recent years. In 2009, an all-time high of 165 charges of *lèse-majesté* were sent to the Court of First Instance.

LYRICS TO ONE NIGHT IN BANGKOK
· · · · · · ·

Performed by British artist Murray Head and the Swedish singer Anders Glenmark, the chart-topping song "One Night In Bangkok" was released on the 1984 concept album of the musical *Chess*, which made its stage premiere in London in 1986. In Act II of the musical, a chess championship is held in Bangkok. The song's lyrics juxtapose excitement about the city's nightlife with the tamer perspective of a chess player. The song was banned in Thailand in 1985.

One night in Bangkok makes a hard man humble
Not much between despair and ecstasy
One night in Bangkok and the tough guys tumble
Can't be too careful with your company
I can feel the devil walking next to me

Bangkok, Oriental setting
And the city don't know what the city is getting
The crème de la crème of the chess world
In a show with everything but Yul Brynner

Time flies, doesn't seem a minute
Since the Tirolean Spa had the chess boys in it
All change, don't you know that when you
Play at this level, there's no ordinary venue

It's Iceland or the Philippines
Or Hastings or, or this place
One night in Bangkok and the world's your oyster
The bars are temples but the pearls ain't free
You'll find a God in every golden cloister

And if you're lucky then the God's a she
I can feel an angel sliding up to me

One town's very like another
When your head's down over your pieces, Brother

It's a drag, it's a bore, it's really such a pity
To be looking at the board, not looking at the city

Whaddya mean?
Ya seen one crowded, polluted, stinking town

Tea girls, warm and sweet, warm, sweet
Some are set up in the Somerset Maugham Suite

"Get Thai'd", you're talking to a tourist
Whose every move's among the purest
I get my kicks above the waistline, sunshine

One night in Bangkok makes a hard man humble
Not much between despair and ecstasy
One night in Bangkok and the tough guys tumble
Can't be too careful with your company
I can feel the devil walking next to me

Siam's gonna be the witness
To the ultimate test of cerebral fitness
This grips me more than would
A muddy old river or Reclining Buddha

But thank God, I'm only watching the game,
controlling it

I don't see you guys rating
The kind of mate I'm contemplating
I'd let you watch, I would invite you
But the queens we use would not excite you

So you better go back to your bars, your temples
Your massage parlours

One night in Bangkok and the world's your oyster
The bars are temples but the pearls ain't free
You'll find a God in every golden cloister
A little flesh, a little history
I can feel an angel slidin' up to me

One night in Bangkok makes a hard man humble
Not much between despair and ecstasy
One night in Bangkok and the tough guys tumble
Can't be too careful with your company
I can feel the devil walking next to me

HOW TO GIVE ALMS
· · · · · · ·

B uddhist monks usually leave the temple at 5am to receive alms from the public and return before 7am to consume the breakfast. The food can only be kept until 11am.

Some guidelines regarding the giving of alms:

1. Before the monks arrive, the giver should raise the food items above his or her head and make a wish.

2. The monk will only stop if asked so the giver must request the passing monk to receive alms.

3. The giver then takes off his or her shoes.

4. When the monk opens the lid of his bowl, the giver puts the food items into the bowl, starting with rice.

5. When finished, the giver puts his or her palms together in a *wai* posture, and stands lower than the monk or sits on his or her knees, while the monk offers blessings in Pali-Sanskit.

TEN HIGHEST COMPANY INCOMES IN 2010
· · · · · · ·

	Company	Income
1	PTT	1,943.85 billon baht
2	Siam Cement Group (SCG)	334.12 billion baht
3	Thai Oil	324.35 billion baht
4	PTT Aromatics and Refining (PTTAR)	277.31 billion baht
5	IRPC	223.80 billon baht
6	Charoen Pokphand Foods (CPF)	195.05 billion baht
7	Thai Airways International	184.27 billion baht
8	Esso (Thailand)	179.74 billion baht
9	PTT Exploration and Production (PTTEP)	147.57 billion baht
10	CP ALL	141.03 billion baht

Source: *Manager* magazine

THE LIGHTER SIDE OF SPYING DURING WWII
• • • • • • •

During World War II, local officials, the underground and foreign spies operated right under the noses of the Japanese occupying troops.

Thanks to the Thais, American OSS officers were billeted in the Rose Garden Palace, a riverside royal residence. Less than 100 metres from Japanese soldiers, agents operated radios and met with other spies. One particularly valuable Thai agent who lunched almost daily with Japanese officers was noted for his punctuality at the palace's follow-up sundowner.

Though they suspected an underground operated and had even captured some OSS (precursor to the CIA) agents, the Japanese were so taken by the friendliness of the Thais they never suspected the magnitude of the secrets hidden behind the smiles. The Thais also proved extremely creative at solving problems.

When one of the first OSS agents in Thailand began to crack under the strain of his work with his Thai hosts, the Thais evacuated an entire neighbourhood and installed eight women in a safe house to provide companionship and help him recover. Launches from the Thai Customs Department often ferried spies and POWs between Bangkok and amphibious planes flown into the Gulf of Siam.

In one case, an American POW held in Bangkok was to feign illness so Thai guards could "take him to hospital". If the Japanese questioned his absence, the Thais would say he had died and been cremated in line with local customs. When this plan was thought too risky, the head of the Thai police concocted an elegant ruse using a "forged" release notice to absolve him and the camp head of responsibility for the escape.

To help resupply Thai hospitals, a huge crowd was assembled to see Thai soldiers stage a fancy drill outside the Royal Palace. As air-raid sirens sounded, fighters swooped menacingly low and bombers parachuted supplies into the park. Amidst the pandemonium of this "attack", the unruly crowd fought over some supplies and the underground spirited off the rest, leaving the embarrassed Japanese looking utterly incompetent.

Source: Studies in Intelligence, The OSS Society

A GROWING PROBLEM
• • • • • • •

- 17 million Thais are classified as obese
- Thailand is ranked as having the 5th highest rate of obesity in the Asia-Pacific region
- A study in 1962 found that Thais consumed 18 grammes of fat per day. The latest study in 2000 found that Thai people consumed 42 to 45 grammes of fat daily
- People in the northeastern region had the least number of obese people compared to other regions

Source: Department of Health report "Thai Health 2011"

Q & A WITH ANAND PANYARACHUN
• • • • • • •

Thailand's prime minister twice in the 1990s, Anand Panyarachun was born in 1932, educated in England, and spent over two decades in the foreign service.

Nickname? I am one of the very few Thais without a nickname. Being the youngest child in a family of 12, I suppose my parents ran out of names.
Favourite musicians? I used to listen to quite a lot of opera with my father. Today, I listen mostly to 50s music. I also like the singer Sarah Brightman.
Favourite sports to play? Tennis and squash.
Favourite tennis player of all-time? Roger Federer.
Favourite sports teams? Boston Bruins in the National Hockey League, for football Barcelona, and the Thai women's national volleyball team.
Favourite films? *Gone with the Wind* and *Four Weddings and a Funeral*.
Favourite actress? Meryl Streep.
Favourite writers? Thomas Hardy and Somerset Maugham.
Favourite drink or cocktail? Malt whiskey.

Source: Interview by *Thailand at Random* editors, 10 September 2012

LIFE IS NOT SUFFERING, IN THAILAND AT LEAST
• • • • • • •

A survey by Gallup conducted in 146 countries and released in 2012 sought to classify respondents as either "thriving", "struggling" or "suffering" based on how they rated their current lives and future prospects. The 0–10 scale revealed that around 13% of the world's population was "suffering". Respondents did not label themselves as "suffering" but a score of under 4 classified them as such. Interestingly, Thais were considered the second least suffering people in the world. This did not mean they were necessarily "thriving", but only Brazilians were classified as suffering less.

The countries with the least "suffering" people in the world:
Brazil – less than 1%
Thailand – 1%
Canada – 1%
Luxembourg – 1%
The Netherlands – 1%

The countries with the most "suffering" people in the world:
Bulgaria – 45%
Yemen – 38%
Armenia – 35%
El Salvador – 33%
Nepal – 31%

Source: www.gallup.com

COMMON DISH CALORIE COUNTER
· · · · · · ·

Dish	Calories
Pad Thai with egg	670
sen yai pat si eiw (fried wheat noodles)	635
hoy maeng pu tot sai kai (fried mussels with egg)	525
khao man kai (rice with steamed chicken)	500
khao phat ka pow kai (rice with stir-fried chicken and holy basil leaves)	495
sen yai ratna moo (fried wheat noodles with pork in gravy)	450
khao moo daeng (rice with roasted pork)	445
kanom chin nam ya (rice noodles with fish-based curry)	430
ka po pla (Chinese-style fish belly soup)	300
kuay tiew sen lek nam (wheat noodles in soup)	365
kuay chap (Chinese wheat noodles with pork and entrails in soup)	295
por pia sot (fresh spring rolls)	180
chok moo (pork congee)	175
pa tong go tot (deep-fried dough)	140
salapao sai moo (steamed pork buns)	80

Source: The Institute of Nutrition, Mahidol University and Phyathai Hospital

HOW TO SPOT A FAKE LOTTERY TICKET
· · · · · · ·

If you want to try your luck, stay away from shady vendors, and at least know the basic characteristics of a legitimate lottery ticket.

- The texture of the paper is smooth, resilient and very thin. It also has a yellowish tint.
- When you hold the lottery ticket up to sunlight, you should be able to see the *Vayupak* watermark clearly.
- There are two types of thread used in the paper: threads you can see and those you cannot. You need ultraviolet light to see the concealed threads (they will glow).
- Real lottery tickets are coated with chemicals. A drop of benzene oil or Haiter bleach will create a ring stain. If no reaction takes place, the ticket is a forgery.

Source: The Government Lottery Office

BEFORE WIKILEAKS: AN AMBASSADOR DOESN'T MINCE WORDS
· · · · · · ·

Sir Anthony Rumbold, British ambassador to Thailand from 1965 to 1967, reported back to Her Britannic Majesty's government on 18 July 1967 before leaving his post. Some excerpts from his free-wheeling communiqué:

"The general level of intelligence of the Thais is rather low, a good deal lower than ours and much lower than that of the Chinese. But there are a few very intelligent and articulate ones and I have often tried to get some of these with whom I believe myself to be on close terms to come clean with me and to describe their national characteristics as they see them themselves and to explain why they behave in this way ...

"It is moreover extraordinary how little the average citizen of Bangkok knows at first hand about the rest of his country. Those who can afford to travel for pleasure go to Europe and America. Apart from occasional visits to seaside resorts or to Chiengmai which has a certain snob appeal they do not dream of travelling in any other part of the country. They are simply not interested ...

"He [the peasant] even looks better dressed than he did two years ago. New roads and irrigation schemes bring him unlooked-for benefits however slowly. He is not interested in ideas or does not care much one way or the other about what happens in Bangkok. He has a vague feeling of loyalty to the King. He is almost impervious to political propaganda ...

"When I caught a glimpse of it [Bangkok] in 1955 it was a pretty place of canals and trees and scarlet-in-gold temples. It is now fast becoming one of the ugliest towns in the world, indistinguishable from the meaner parts of Tokyo or Los Angeles. But there have been no corresponding changes in the habits or attitudes of the inhabitants though there are of course many more of them ...

"The foreigner must not try to unravel and define them [the Thais] in all their complexity because the task is too difficult. The best he can do is to try to understand the general rules by which they seem to be established ...

"I have enjoyed living for a while in Thailand ... It is true that they have no literature, no painting and only a very odd kind of music, but their sculpture, their ceramics and their dancing are borrowed from others and that their architecture is monotonous and their interior decoration hideous ... And if anybody wants to know what their culture consists of the answer is that it consists of themselves, their excellent manners, their fastidious habits, their graceful gestures and their elegant persons. If we are elephants and oxen they are gazelles and butterflies."

Source: Sir Anthony Rumbold's *Goodbye to Thailand* classified communiqué, 18 July 1967

A SMILE FOR EVERY OCCASION
· · · · · · ·

The supposed trademark of Thailand: smiling. But if Thailand is the "Land of Smiles", you should know there are many kinds of smiles (*yim*). Try to decode what you see in real life with some help from the table below.

Name of smile	What it means
Yim thak tai	A courteous, welcoming smile
Yim chuen chom	An admiring smile
Yim fuen fuen	A fake smile
Yim mi let nai	A plotting smile
Yim yo	A condescending smile
Yim yae yae	A sheepish smile
Yim sao	A sad-looking smile
Yim haeng haeng or *yim chuean chuean*	A dry (forced) smile
Yim su	A spirited smile

Source: *The Cornerstones of Thai Society-Relationships and Hierarchy*

BUY PHUKET FOR 120 MILLION BAHT
· · · · · · ·

Board game junkies who want to play the hit investment game, Monopoly, with a local twist will be thrilled to hear that there is a locally produced version, known in Thai as the "Millionaire Game" in which the properties are named after different provinces. The cheapest is Krabi province, which sells for 60 million baht and the most expensive is Bangkok, at 400 million baht. Two train stations, Hat Yai and Korat, can also be purchased. One of the special player pieces exclusive to this version is a Thai-style train.

The price list for some of the major provinces:

Songkhla .... 60 million baht
Surat Thani .... 100 million baht
Phuket .... 120 million baht
Nong Khai .... 140 million baht
Loei .... 150 million baht
Ubon Ratchatani .... 180 million baht
Khon Kaen .... 200 million baht

Sukhothai .... 220 million baht
Tak .... 220 million baht
Mae Hong Son .... 280 million baht
Kanchanaburi .... 300 million baht
Ayutthaya .... 300 million baht
Rayong .... 320 million baht
Chon Buri .... 350 million baht

SIZE MATTERS
· · · · · ·

- Thailand is the 50th largest country in the world
- It is similar in size to Spain, France and Texas
- It covers an area of approximately 514,000 sq km (200,000 sq miles), including 2,230 sq km of water
- The length of Thailand's total coastline is 3,219 km
- The longest shared border is with Myanmar, stretching around 1,800 km

Source: Tourism Authority of Thailand

ANIMAL OMENS: THE MEANING OF THE BIRDS AND THE BEES
· · · · · · ·

Good omen	Bad omen
Bees build a beehive in the house	A gecko makes noise during the daytime
Wild animals come onto your property (arriving from the north or west)	Wild animals come onto your property (from the south or east)
Dogs bite each other in the house	A black cat or another black animal walks by you (from right to left) before you leave the house
Another person's dog runs from its owner into your house	A crow appears
A toad hops up the stairs	An abandoned dog stays in your house
A bat flies into the room	Black ants form a trail into your house
A horse runs into the house	A dog chases a cat into the house and they fight
A sparrow makes a nest in the house	A cat chases a dog into the house and they fight
A snake leaves its skin in the house	There is a bullfrog in the kitchen

KEY CHARACTERS OF THE RAMAKIEN
. . . .

Thailand's national epic, called the *Ramakien*, was adapted directly from the Hindu epic, the *Ramayana*. The story is traditionally told through the costumed dance performance *khon* and features four types of characters: male, female, demons and simian. There are 311 characters in the *Ramakien*. The main characters are:

- Phra Ram (or Rama) – the righteous king of Ayudhya
- Phra Lak (or Lakshman) – Phra Ram's loyal brother
- Sita – Phra Ram's beautiful consort
- Hanuman – loyal simian general of Phra Ram
- Totsakanth – ten-faced and twenty-armed evil king of Longka
- Phipek – a prophet and the brother of Totsakanth, he was expelled after prophesying that Totsakanth would be killed by Phra Ram. Phipek later joined the army of Phra Ram under the king of Longka after the death of Totsakanth.

Most of the epic focuses on the war waged between Phra Ram and Totsakanth.

MEMBERS ONLY
. . . .

The Royal Bangkok Sports Club (RBSC) is Thailand's most exclusive members-only club. It has its origins in the Bangkok Gymkhana Club and today occupies prime real estate in the centre of the capital. Anchored by an 18-hole golf course that is surrounded by a horseracing track, the club also features tennis courts (including grass ones), lawn bowling, swimming pools, and more. Every other Sunday, the RBSC hosts horse races, which are open to the general public. Apart from the government lottery, betting on horses is one of very few legal forms of gambling in Thailand. The waiting list to become a full-fledged member of the RBSC has been closed for years. Now only the sons and daughters of existing members are able to join, with an initial membership fee of a reported 2 million baht.

Timeline:
- 1901 – The RBSC is founded under the patronage of His Majesty King Chulalongkorn
- 1903 – Horse racing commences at the RBSC
- 1911 – The RBSC becomes Thailand's first airport when demonstration flights of the first aircraft to arrive in Thailand take off from its grounds
- 1926 – King Prajadhipok becomes the first Thai ruler to play a round of golf at the RBSC
- 1941 – The Imperial Japanese Army occupies the club in December
- 1941 – *Mom Chao* Rachada Bhisek Sonakul becomes the first Thai chairman of the RBSC
- 1985 – Twelve-year-old Tiger Woods competes at the RBSC

Sources: The Royal Bangkok Sports Club, Asian Racing Federation, CNNGo.com

ACCOUNT OF ALLIED BOMBINGS IN BANGKOK
· · · · · · ·

"On 5 June 1944 (*Visakha Bucha* Day) at 11am near the Memorial Bridge, Mr Ajin and his friend saw Allied bombers flying in circles. They saw white smoke coming off the bomber wings. At first, they thought that the bomber was hit by anti-aircraft guns. The bomber circled and flew away a few seconds later. Its purpose was to mark the target area with smoke for the rest of the fleet. Then a fleet of B29 bombers poured iron eggs (bombs) aiming to destroy the Memorial Bridge and Wat Liab Power Plant. However, they hit buildings around Tha Tian and Ban Moh area instead! The power line for the tram (a pair of copper wires about the size of a thumb) was cut by the shrapnel. The buildings around Ban Moh intersection turned to debris, obstructing the tram services from Bang Lamphoo to Hua Lamphong via Ban Moh. However, the tram lines from Pahurat, Ratchawongse pier, Song Wat area, Sam Yaek and Hua Lamphong still functioned. The bombs destroyed a Japanese hospital in Ban Moh and corpses were scattered around the area. Mr Ajin survived the bombardment even though a bomb dropped ten metres away from him. After that day, schools and universities in Bangkok were closed and moved out of Bangkok for safety and the workers from Wat Liab Power Plant came to reconnect the torn copper wires and repair the tracks a few days later. B29s arrived again on 14 April 1945 and plunged Bangkok into darkness as Wat Liab and Samsen Power Plant were destroyed, tap water was cut off, there was no light from light bulbs, roads turned dark after sunset, and the trams were not running. It took four to five years to get everything back to normal."

Source: Ajin Panjaphan, a famous writer who founded *Fah Muang Thai* weekly magazine, as reproduced on www.2bangkok.com

THE TEN VOWS OF BUDDHIST MONKS
· · · · · · ·

Buddhist monks proclaim ten vows during their ordination ceremony:

"I take the vow not to destroy life."
"I take the vow not to steal."
"I take the vow to abstain from impurity."
"I take the vow not to lie."
"I take the vow not to eat at forbidden times."
"I take the vow to abstain from dancing, singing, music and stage plays."
"I take the vow not to use garlands, scents, unguents, or ornaments."
"I take the vow not to use a board of high bed."
"I take the vow not to receive gold or silver."

THE MORE THINGS CHANGE ...

The following editorial appeared in the *Bangkok Post* in 1955:

RUMORS

Bangkok periodically is filled with rumors, and this is one of those periods. There are rumors of plots against the Government, of Government-Military-Police plans to arrest National Assemblymen and journalists, and of various other startling things. There are even counter-rumors by accused persons that the original rumors were really started by the seeming targets of the rumors or as to make the accused look like wicked rumormongers. It gets very devious at times.

While some of the rumors may have elements of truth in them, it is doubtful that many members of the general public believe them. It would seem that the rumormongers themselves must realize this by now. However, many of the rumors are news, even if false, because of the motives behind their spreading. Whether it is meant to gain personal publicity, to discredit an enemy, to try to create excitement, or something worse, the initiating of a false rumor can be dangerous to the initiator, when a skeptical public reacts not by believing but by speculating why the rumor is spread. Therefore, one wonders if the current rumormongers would not be wiser, and more prudent, if they avoided over-working this device at the present time when the public has heard "wolf" cried so often that it would hardly believe a true rumor any more.

THE WINE MARKET

- An estimated 10% of Thais drink wine
- Wine comprises 3% of the alcohol beverage market in Thailand
- Red wine has a 70% market share in Thailand's wine retail market
- The most popular grape varietals are Cabernet Sauvignon, Shiraz, Merlot and Pinot Noir respectively
- Low to medium-priced level wines (below US$40) hold the biggest market share
- Thailand has fewer than ten local wine producers and the retail price of these wines starts at US$6 per bottle
- The price for better Thai wine can be over US$20 per bottle. They are viewed as competition to imported wines.
- Most wines consumed in Thailand are imported from France, Australia, Italy, Chile and the US.
- The total import value of wine in 2008 was US$33 million.

Source: Global Agricultural Information Network's report in 2009

FAQ ABOUT THE KING
· · · · · · ·

The Ministry of Foreign Affairs launched a website thailandtoday.org as a "one-stop source of comprehensive and reliable facts and information about Thailand". As of September 2012, the website listed frequently asked questions about the Thai monarchy as listed below. The Foreign Ministry's answers to these questions are available on the website.

1. What is the role of the Thai monarch?
2. Why do Thais love their king?
3. Has the Thai monarchy involved itself in politics?
4. Has the king given his implied blessing to coups staged in the name of stability and clean government?
5. What is the *lèse-majesté* law in Thailand?
6. Does the *lèse-majesté* law undermine democracy and limit freedom of expression?
7. Why has the *lèse-majesté* law become an issue of criticism? Has it been used as a tool for prosecution of political opponents?
8. What has been done to alleviate the aforementioned problem?
9. Who can amend the law?
10. There have been concerns over possible implications [*sic*] that royal succession might have on political stability. Is there any cause for such concern?
11. Is it accurate that the Thai monarchy is the world's richest monarch [*sic*]?

Source: www.thailandtoday.org

HOW DOES LIFE COMPARE?
· · · · · · ·

Country	Thailand	Regional average	Global average
Male life expectancy (years)	66	64	66
Female life expectancy (years)	74	67	71
Population living in urban areas (%)	34	32	50
Prevalence of HIV (per 1000 adults aged 15–49)	13	3	8
Adult mortality rate (probability of dying between 15–60 years per 1000 population)	205	209	176

Source: World Health Organization (updated May 2012)

CHIPS OFF THE OLD BLOCK
· · · · · · ·

Potato chips (crisps) are very popular among Thais. In order to cater to Thai taste buds and mimic popular dishes from Thai cuisine, manufacturers have created unique flavours for the local market. Some potato chip flavours include:

- Crispy basil
- Grilled squid with hot chilli sauce
- Peking duck
- Hot and spicy crab
- Bacon and seaweed baked with cheese
- *Nam prik pao* (Thai hot chilli paste)
- Salmon teriyaki

- Soft shell crab with garlic and pepper sauce
- Seaweed and prawn tempura
- Chicken *num tok* (northeastern-style spicy salad)
- Curry-powdered crab

HIJACKINGS
· · · · · · ·

- On 28 March 1973, a suspected communist hijacked a bus and drove it to Don Muang airport, where he demanded an airplane. However, he couldn't decide on a destination. First he chose Moscow, then Beijing, and finally Hong Kong. In the end, he ended up nowhere as security forces surrounded the bus and took him into custody.

- On 31 March 1981, five Indonesians hijacked a domestic airplane and flew to Bangkok's Don Muang airport. They demanded the release of political prisoners and another plane to Sri Lanka. After holding passengers hostage for three days, the hijackers were overwhelmed by Thai and Indonesian commandos, who stormed the plane, killing three of the hijackers and capturing two others in an eight-minute raid.

- On 1 July 1981, a Sri Lankan who claimed to have explosives strapped to his body hijacked a plane and landed at Don Muang airport, where his demands for $300,000 and a reunion with his wife and child were granted.

- On 18 January 1983, three Thai men hijacked a plane from Lampang and directed it toward Chiang Rai. They were told the plane needed to refuel and needed to land in Chiang Mai. When the plane landed, the captain and co-pilot locked the cockpit and jumped out, while two flight attendants and some passengers fled through a rear door. Eventually, the hijackers escaped in a military police pick-up as the hostages were released.

- On 6 October 1989, two Burmese students hijacked a plane from Mergui to Thailand and demanded the release of political prisoners. After receiving no response from the Burmese government, the hijackers surrendered after 11 hours but were able to voice their pro-democracy views to news reporters.

STUMBLING INTO HISTORY
. . . .

C onsidered the most important prehistoric settlement found so far in Southeast Asia, Ban Chiang in Thailand's northeastern region was discovered, in part, by accident. The ancient civilisation, which presents the earliest evidence of farming in the region as well as the manufacture and use of metals, may never have been discovered had Harvard undergraduate Steve Young, who was researching his honours thesis there, not lost his footing. One day while walking down a village path with his local assistant, Young stumbled over a root and fell flat on his face. Under him were the exposed lids of pottery jars. The pieces, which had been exposed by erosion, featured striking designs and colours. Young noticed that the fragments were not glazed, and so must have been very old.

After Young's discovery in 1966, archaeologists from the Fine Arts Department of Thailand and the University of Pennsylvania Museum of Archaeology and Anthropology teamed up to begin excavations at Ban Chiang. During the first formal scientific excavation in 1967, several skeletons, together with bronze "grave gifts", were unearthed. Rice fragments have also been found, leading to the conclusion that the Bronze Age settlers were probably farmers. The site's oldest graves do not include bronze artefacts and are therefore from a Neolithic culture; the most recent graves date to the Iron Age.

The first dating of the artefacts using the thermoluminescence technique suggested they originated as far back as 4420 BC to 3400 BC, which would have made the site the earliest Bronze Age culture in the world. However, after the 1974–75 excavation, sufficient material became available for radiocarbon dating, which resulted in more recent dates. The earliest grave is believed to date from about 2100 BC, while the latest dates from about 200 AD.

Sources: UNESCO, Penn Museum website

A SIAMESE SOLDIER IN THE AMERICAN CIVIL WAR
. . . .

J oining the Union Army on 12 August 1862 was a short, 18-year-old man who had travelled all the way from Siam to fight in the American Civil War. He was listed as George Dupont but his real name is believed to have been "Yod" or "Tor". He served in the 13th New Jersey Volunteers for a year and took part in three major battles, including Gettysburg. In 1865 he was discharged and four years later became an American citizen in Philadelphia, before returning to Thailand in 1870.

Sources: *The Eagle and The Elephant: 100 Years of Thai-American Relations* and *Siam's Union Army Veteran* by William F. Strobridge

THE AMULET COLLECTOR'S DREAM

Talismans and Buddhist amulets are worn by some Thais in order to bring them good luck or prevent bad luck, or protect them from evil spells. Some collectors strive to collect *bencha phaki*, the holy grail set of the following five expensive and popular amulets.

1. *Somdet wat rakang* – approximate market price is 10–35 million baht (US$320,000–$1,120,000)

2. *Phra sumkor* – approximate market price is 1.5–9 million baht (US$48,000–$288,000)

3. *Phra nang phya* – approximate market price is 200,000–5 million baht (US$6,400–$160,000)

4. *Phra pongsuphan* – approximate market price is 200,000–5 million baht (US$6,400–$160,000)

5. *Phra rod* – approximate market price is 250,000–10 million baht (US$8,000–$320,000)

Source: www.talad-pra.com

SOME PRICES DURING THE GREAT FLOOD OF 1942

A pair of shoes made from rubber tires	35 satang
A durian	100 baht
A prostitute at Soi Sub	10–20 baht
A prostitute at Chaloemkrung	10–20 baht
Monthly salary for Bangkok dock worker	50 baht

Source: Ajin Panjaphan, a famous writer who founded *Fah Muang Thai* weekly magazine

FAVOURITE CARS TO STEAL

The 2010 police report on stolen vehicles in the Bangkok area shows that Toyota vehicles were the most frequently jacked, followed by Isuzus and then Nissans. Among motorcycles, Hondas were the most commonly stolen, followed by Yamahas and Kawasakis. Thieves were reported to be the most active between 8pm and midnight.

Source: www.khaosod.com

HOW TO MAKE MERIT
· · · · · · ·

W hen visiting a Buddhist temple with the intention of making merit, many types of donations can be made, from money to more long-lasting life "essentials" such as toiletries. This latter offering is known as *sangkatan*. This offering is often made in the form of a container filled with useful commodities such as dried food, soap, toothpaste, razors and medical supplies. The container typically used in Thailand is a yellow plastic bucket. People can buy pre-stocked containers at most supermarkets and shops. Some make their own *sangkatan*.

When offering a *sangkatan* to a monk (or monks), a specific ritual must be followed.

1. The original idea of *sangkatan* is that the objects are not intended for a specific monk but whichever monk you encounter.
2. If you arrive at the temple later than 11am you must exclude any food items.
3. Light two candles and three incense sticks in front of the Buddha statues to pay respect to the Buddha, the *dhamma* (Buddhist teachings) and the *sangha* (Buddhist clergy).
4. Give prayers in Pali (and Thai in some cases) requesting the five precepts and receive them through the monk's chanting.
5. Chant more prayers specifically in regards to this offering of *sangkatan*, specific recipients can also be mentioned (yourself, your family, spirits of deceased relatives or loved ones, spirits with no relatives or enemies from former lives).
6. The monk will then receive the offerings (for women, the monk will have to extend his robe to accept the offerings as he cannot touch a woman). Money can also be given by putting it in an envelope as part of the offering.
7. To finish the process, you will offer a libation—by pouring water from one container into another—to dedicate the merit to the departed while the monk chants. When the chanting reaches the word *yata* all the water in the container must be poured into the second container. After that, pour the water onto the root of any big tree in the area.
8. Before leaving, pay respect to the monk by prostrating yourself and *krab* (a gesture similar to the *wai* with the additional act of placing both palms onto the ground) three times.

SIAMESE ENVOYS TO FRANCE
· · · · · · ·

T he first Siamese legation to France was sent in 1681 but was lost at sea. The next one arrived in 1684 and successfully requested that a French mission be sent to the capital at that time, Ayudhya. This French mission arrived in 1685 and then returned to France with three Thai ambassadors and an entourage of more than 40 people. On arrival in 1686, the Thai mission received an audience with King Louis XIV at Versailles.

INDEX